1,000,000 Books
are available to read at

Forgotten Books

www.ForgottenBooks.com

Read online
Download PDF
Purchase in print

ISBN 978-1-332-01616-7
PIBN 10269220

This book is a reproduction of an important historical work. Forgotten Books uses state-of-the-art technology to digitally reconstruct the work, preserving the original format whilst repairing imperfections present in the aged copy. In rare cases, an imperfection in the original, such as a blemish or missing page, may be replicated in our edition. We do, however, repair the vast majority of imperfections successfully; any imperfections that remain are intentionally left to preserve the state of such historical works.

Forgotten Books is a registered trademark of FB &c Ltd.
Copyright © 2018 FB &c Ltd.
FB &c Ltd, Dalton House, 60 Windsor Avenue, London, SW19 2RR.
Company number 08720141. Registered in England and Wales.

For support please visit www.forgottenbooks.com

1 MONTH OF FREE READING

at
www.ForgottenBooks.com

By purchasing this book you are eligible for one month membership to ForgottenBooks.com, giving you unlimited access to our entire collection of over 1,000,000 titles via our web site and mobile apps.

To claim your free month visit:
www.forgottenbooks.com/free269220

* Offer is valid for 45 days from date of purchase. Terms and conditions apply.

English
Français
Deutsche
Italiano
Español
Português

www.forgottenbooks.com

Mythology Photography **Fiction** Fishing Christianity **Art** Cooking Essays Buddhism Freemasonry Medicine **Biology** Music **Ancient Egypt** Evolution Carpentry Physics Dance Geology **Mathematics** Fitness Shakespeare **Folklore** Yoga Marketing **Confidence** Immortality Biographies Poetry **Psychology** Witchcraft Electronics Chemistry History **Law** Accounting **Philosophy** Anthropology Alchemy Drama Quantum Mechanics Atheism Sexual Health **Ancient History Entrepreneurship** Languages Sport Paleontology Needlework Islam **Metaphysics** Investment Archaeology Parenting Statistics Criminology **Motivational**

History and Genealogy

OF

A BRANCH OF THE FAMILY OF KINNE

BY

EMERSON KINNE.

SYRACUSE, N. Y.
MASTERS & STONE, PRINTERS AND BINDERS.
1881.

Gc
929.2
K623k
1159772

INTRODUCTION.

Having, for a number of years, a desire to learn something of the ancestry of the Kinnes of Onondaga County, the writer of the following glance sketches, has, after considerable time, some correspondence, with a measure of trouble and patient investigation, obtained the facts herein recorded.

At the outset he may be permitted the expression of a candid sentiment that he has been impelled to this pleasant and yet somewhat difficult undertaking, more by a desire to snatch from unmerited, but inevitable oblivion, the facts, incidents and personal histories of our kinsmen, who are fast passing from the scenes that make history, to the unknown and unending future, than by an undue or personal family pride.

If, in the faithful record of facts, found in these pages, there shall appear any merit attaching itself to deeds of daring, or of patriotism, or of patient submission, where submission was a virtue, or of Christian zeal and labor, or of the more common virtues in humbler walks of life, such merit may be grateful to any of the kindred, whose eye may chance to rest on this humble attempt to record and preserve some of their history.

Such is my admiration of the virtue and heroism of our

forefathers, the early settlers of New England, such my veneration for their loyalty to God and their country, so marvelous do I count their hardships and sufferings, in their early attempts to colonize, their almost obstinate persistence in meeting and surmounting difficulties and their rigid practice of the primitive virtues; that my kinsmen will, perhaps, accord with my desire to lay before them some of the causes and considerations underlying the settlement and colonization of New England.

To this end I invited my nephew, Edward D. Kinne, of Ann Arbor, Michigan, son of my oldest brother, Julius C. Kinne, to prepare a paper on that subject, to be read at a probable re-union of Kinnes, to be held in Cortland, N. Y., to accompany this record.

In compliance with my request, he has paused in his busy pursuit of legal and legislative duties, and sent me what would seem to be, a suitable and proper introduction to the history of any family of the descendants of New England.

It has been said, that if our Pilgrim Fathers had settled on the western shores of America, instead of on the eastern, the eastern shores would still have been in the possession of the Indian race.

Whether there be any truth in this, or whether it be only a mere waggish way of lauding our wide western domains, is of little consequence.

One thing is certain; had a less hardy and heroic people encountered the trials which they did, New England had made quite another history, than that she has. Glorious as it is, she has shaped the history and directed the destiny of other, if not all other sections of the country.

Salem, the seat and center of settlements, next to Plymouth, was the first town settled in Massachusetts.

The first church organization effected in this country was at Salem, in 1629.

Witchcraft flourished and died here.

In the revolutionary war 158 privateers, mounting 2,000 guns, manned by 6,000 men were fitted out from this town.

Salem has a history. And from this place the name of Kinne, in the person of Henry, originates, as seen in the record.

The very sterility of New England soil, and the inclemency of its climate stimulated industry and incited to emigration, and its tide has ever after been westward.

Henry's descendants, scattered over various parts of New England, were not behind in enterprise, or purposes of permanent improvement in their material interests.

It is presumably known to all, that, by grant and subsequent purchase, Stephen Van Rensselaer, called the "Patroon," was the proprietor of about three-fourths of a million of acres of land, comprising the greater part of the present counties of Albany, Columbia and Rensselaer,—that he was the liberal landlord of the occupants of these lands, requiring only a mere nominal rent, leasing on long time, in some cases ninety-nine years. Such inducements, naturally invited emigration thither, and Cyrus Kinne, fourth in line from Henry Kinne, was induced to leave Voluntown, Conn., and settle on leased land in Rensselaer county. Enterprise and adventure know but little of limits. When once they have impelled men to strike out for independence, ease or affluence, every new promise of good, discovers avenues, penetrates forests, divides waters, bridges rivers, braves dangers, achieves victories and secures success.

Central New York, by a very generous provision of the

state and national governments, became in 1783 an objective point, by the disposition and distribution of public lands. There is now in the possession of Allen B. Kinne, of Woodard, Onondaga County, N. Y., an original deed of conveyance, to Cyrus Kinne, Esq., of one hundred acres of land from the State of New York, when John Jay was Governor, and Lewis A. Scott, Secretary of State. The deed bears date Sept. 2, 1795, and has attached to it the Great Seal of the State, which consists of a piece of wax, circular in form, three inches in diameter, and nearly a half inch in thickness, covered with parchment, bearing the impress, " The Great Seal of the State," and " Excelsior," and on the reverse, " Frustra," "1777." This was only one of the many parcels purchased.

These lands lying in the central part of the State constitute what was called the " Military Tract." Their cheapness and fertility soon became known.

A clear exposition of the status of this "tract" was published some time since in the columns of the *Syracuse Journal*, and is deemed of sufficient interest to be laid before our friends.

I desire to thank those who have responded to inquiries, in pursuance of the work I have had in hand, without whose aid, the task would have been fraught with greater difficulties and its results less satisfactory.

In the work undertaken, I have been assisted by my brother, A. E. Kinne, to whom I have often had occasion to refer, and to whom I desire herein to acknowledge my obligations.

In the Record I have attempted, it was my purpose, in the beginning, simply to place in manuscript form, such facts concerning the Onondaga branch of Kinnes, as were clearly in my own memory.

But as these were recorded, other facts and incidents, not distinctly remembered, but standing in such close relation to those well remembered, that some correspondence became indispensable to anything like a perfect and impartial recital of what was recalled.

The object of the work was to leave in some tangible form, what my immediate kinsmen might wish to preserve, and to place at the service of any one or more of them who would wish to perfect and extend the record and genealogy so as to include others or all of the name of Kinne, who now live or have lived in this country.

As the work grew, and some of our friends desired a more permanent form for preservation, than manuscript, it was deemed more satisfactory and more easy of reference, to put in pamphlet form, what at first was designed only for family reference.

NEW ENGLAND AND NEW ENGLANDERS

SOMETHING OF THEIR HISTORY ; THEIR STRUGGLES, AND THE FRUITION OF THEIR LABORS.

It is foreign to the design of this brief address, to attempt a detailed or elaborate portraiture of our New England ancestry. Such a labor must devolve upon the historian. Ours must be a bird's-eye, philosophical glance at that memorable past. The theme should interest and ennoble every true American heart.

No one, however gifted by nature or versed in modern or classic lore, can speak intelligently or act wisely for his generation, for his country or posterity, unless his eye can light upon, and his memory retain, the salient features of New England history. Wanting in these essential elements of historic knowledge, the American citizen and statesman enters a labyrinth of social, financial and political problems, that the mere logical and philosophical wisdom of man, even aided by the lessons of history, may not hope to fathom or successfully explore.

Plymouth Rock is the polar star of American Liberty! and the political mariner, who pilots his craft, either in ignorance or defiance thereof, may expect shoals and shipwreck.

Fortunately, it is one of the distinguishing characteristics of the human being, that he loves to contemplate the scenes of the past, and that he longs to have his own history borne down to the future.

It is impossible to name a people who do not possess cherished traditions that have descended from their ancestors. The virtues we admire in them not only adorn and dignify their names, but win us to their imitation and emulation.

Their prosperity and happiness spread abroad a diffusive light that reaches us and brightens our condition. The wisdom that guided their footsteps, becomes at the same time, a lamp to our feet; and the observation of the errors of their course, and of the consequent disappointments and sufferings that befell them, enables us to pass in safety through rocks and ledges, on which they were stranded.

The settlement of New England was one of the remote, yet nevertheless, legitimate fruits of that great Religious Reformation of the 16th century; a Reformation thoroughly conceived and inaugurated, when Martin Luther, the intrepid and learned Augustine Monk, in 1517, nailed to the gates of Wittemburg, his famous 95 propositions, which electrified all Germany, and shook to its foundation the whole vast imposing papal edifice.

New England was the diamond spark from the white heat of that religious illumination.

The hymns of love and praise, heard in the 17th century on Plymouth Rock, were the far distant, but perfectly responsive echo of the voice of Luther at the Diet of Worms.

It was his blow at papal supremacy; his voice shouting for Religious Liberty; denouncing indulgencies and the unholy vices of the Church; his system of religious action and thought, that finally changed the foundation of European politics and found their purest crystallization in the moral and civil code, and the enlightened faith of the Pilgrim Fathers of New England.

This precious German seed was soon sown in the hearts of Englishmen, and finally ripened to perfect maturity in the virgin soil of New England. The enfranchisement of the mind from religious despotism culminated in the doctrine of freedom in civil government.

The doctrines of popular liberty found their first life-giving embraces in the wilderness of the newly discovered continent.

Protestantism was a bold advance, a marvelous release from the bondage of the Church of Rome. It struck to the heart the idea of the infallibility of the Pope. It opened thoroughly the avenues of human thought and speculation; and the work went on until mandates from the English throne, upon the subject of religious faith, soon became as powerless to control the minds of Englishmen as the impotent thunders of the Vatican.

Then came the advanced declaration that even the *forms* of the Church of England could not be tolerated;

that not a ceremony should be adopted unless it were enjoined of God. The Bible should be the standard and the rule of action. *Nothing* in *Religion* should be yielded to the Temporal Sovereign. *And this is Puritanism.*

The tale of the sufferings of the early fathers of the Church in England cannot be written here.

The fires of Smithfield that consumed the living martyred bodies of Cranmer, Ridley and Hooper, abated not one jot or tittle of the march of religious freedom, nor weakened or shattered the faith of these lovers of God's truth, the Puritan Fathers. No flames could quench their zeal or their devotion to God. "The blood of the martyrs proved the seed of the Church."

As we see frail human nature in the 19th century, it now seems scarcely less than wonderful that human beings were found who refused to yield to the dangers and temptations of that crucial test of human fortitude and faith.

But the strength of heart, body and soul, which bore them upon the waves of that stormy ocean, came not of the flesh but was of Divine inspiration.

Banishment, poverty, and even the bloody gallows of Tyburn were the rewards that English rule offered these Puritan sons and daughters of civil and religious liberty.

Expatriation appeared inevitable. Their native soil of England became the prison house of their souls. No future was ever more dark, more uncertain, or more tempestuous.

This movement of the Puritan Fathers from England contemplated and involved the surrender of rich earthly possessions; the sundering of the ties of kindred; the abandonment of home; of native scenes; the burial of every luxurious hope.

Behind them was home, native land, kindred and stately antiquity. *Before* them, the life of a refugee, poverty, suffering and peradventure, premature or even ignominious death.

Yet they shrank not from the embrace of this ordeal. To remain in England was to dwarf and enslave their souls. In that long night of sorrow, despair and darkness there was no light to guide their footsteps, save the imperishable glory of the star of faith in God and His goodness and power.

Strange as it may seem, these Puritan Fathers saw that star of hope shining over a foreign land, populated with a people of foreign tongue, habits and language.

Far away to Holland they coursed their way, looking for spiritual emancipation. Holland became the temporary asylum of those Puritans who first dared to brave the pitiless storm of exile.

Glancing back at that period of Puritan history, we learn that even their departure from English soil was attended with struggles and shameful embarrassment. Their first attempt was entirely frustrated, and nearly the whole band of this "poor, persecuted flock of Christ," was thrown by English intolerants into an English prison. Yet there was not a stain upon their white souls, or the shadow of a crime against either man or God o'erhanging them. They were finally released but only to be compelled to meet in secret, in the north of England, in an unfrequented heath of Lincolnshire, and to effect a successful departure, after a cowardly 'seizure of helpless women and children and another desperate struggle for life.

Such was the flight of Robinson and Brewster and their followers from the land of their sires. Such were the adieus that England bade to as brave and loyal hearts as ever trod her soil or bit the dust on her fields of battle.

They landed at Amsterdam, and thither flocked the other refugees from English intolerance. The story of their pilgrimage in Holland is mainly interesting, as revealing the humble zeal and fervent love of this people towards God; their single-heartedness and sincere affection one toward another. They were exiles in a strange land; under a foreign sky; among a people of kind but foreign life. There could not be rapid, natural and harmonious assimilation. It is not remarkable that they became restless, and even impatient for a permanent home, where they might erect their altars by their own firesides, and breathe the delicious atmosphere of perfect freedom.

Such a green spot on this beautiful earth Providence seemed to have anticipated and prepared for their weary feet. The voyages, explorations and discoveries of Hudson, of Sir Walter Raleigh and Capt. John Smith, in the New World, filled them with wonder and an insatiable longing! Not indeed in the spirit of speculation, or idle wandering were they stimulated; but in the hope and moved with an inward zeal of advancing the kingdom of Christ in the remote parts of the New World. It was their ambition and aim to act a higher part in the great drama of human life. Hence towards this new field of human action they turned their thoughts and prayers.

Negotiations followed, and arrangements were soon completed, for a voyage to America. Such of the youngest and strongest of these exiled Puritans as freely offered themselves, constituted the members of this remarkable band.

With the sweet melody of christian prayer and the singing of psalms, floating along the shore, the Speedwell and the Mayflower spread their sails over this devoted people, and soon touch the shores of England at Southampton. From this port, on the 6th day of September, 1620, this band, numbering but one hundred souls, embarked on board the Mayflower, and her prow was soon pointing and cutting the waters towards their future home.

Sixty-three long, weary days and nights this bark moved on, tossed at the mercy of a tempestuous ocean, when the harbor of Cape Cod, on the New England shore, extended its sheltering arms.

It is recorded, that, guided by wisdom that seemeth from above, before these Pilgrim strangers landed, they prepared and signed a sacred compact, declaring their loyalty to the Crown, and covenanting to live together in peace and harmony, with equal rights to all; creating thereby a civil body politic.

Here in the plain cabin of the Mayflower, on a bleak and barren coast, with a trackless ocean on the one side, and an unbroken wilderness on the other, wearied and wasted with a long and despairing voyage, on a cheerless November day in 1620, was laid the primal foundations of Constitutional Liberty in North America.

Though safely moored from the dangers of the deep, their perplexities had hardly commenced. Even the place of their settlement was still to be selected. They met no words of greeting or of welcome. There was no Pisgah which they might ascend, and from whose summit they might behold the grandeur of the New World. Snow covered hills and dangerous valleys greeted their eyes at every step. After days of wandering and exploration, these Pilgrim Fathers place their weary feet upon Plymouth Rock, and here they rest from ocean, toil and danger, and plant their colony. The rock that received their footsteps on that stormy December day, has become a sacred landmark in American history. It is the beacon light of Civil Liberty and Independent Religious Worship.

Here we trace the origin of New England. Here was planted that tree of free, independent and equal rights, before man and God, that in after generations spread its gracious branches over the length and breadth of our Republic, and sheltered and saved us in the hour of National peril.

Happy for us that New England received this colony. Happy for us all that the old English institutions were not transplanted on this soil. Happy for us all that these exiled Pilgrims were English Protestants, disciplined by misfortune, skilled by observation and experience; equal in rank and in rights, and bound by no code of laws or rule save that of religion and the public good.

Who can tell what centuries of human joy, life and prosperity hung upon the uncertainties of that ocean voyage. Had the Mayflower sunk in mid-ocean, the tales of fable might now be gathering around our Colonial history.

No one can reasonably doubt that the theories of our government, its stability, its growth, its development, and especially the spirit and character of our civil and religious rights and institutions, may be traced to the landing of our Pilgrim Fathers on Plymouth Rock. God is in history.

Though firmly rooted to the soil of Plymouth, neither the labors nor the sufferings of our Pilgrim Fathers ceased. A new climate, precarious shelter, and a scarcity of food, soon sadly decimated their ranks. Sickness and death were their daily companions. Before the inclement spring had mellowed into the lap of summer, the benevolent Carver, their first governor, and one-half of this little colony were sleeping in their new made graves. Those in health could not properly care for the sick, and it is said, that in this period of greatest distress there were but seven persons able to render assistance. Privation and want followed sickness and death. Men staggered by reason of faintness for want of food. It is recorded, but without perfect authenticity, that at one time these people were reduced to a pint of corn, which being parched and distributed, gave to each five kernels. Not until 1623 did these miseries end or materially lessen. Yet, during all this period of hardship, misery and self-denial, the unswerving confidence of the Pilgrims in the words of Providence remained unshaken.

It was during this period that this little colony made its first treaty of peace, friendship and mutual protection. It was with the Indian Sachem, Massasoit. It is the oldest act of diplomacy recorded in New England, and was sacredly kept for more than half a century.

The trials and vicissitudes of this colony cannot be fully detailed here. Through scenes of gloom and misery these Pilgrim Fathers struggled, opening the way to an asylum for those who would go to the wilderness for the purity of religion or the liberty of conscience. They were the servants of posterity; the benefactors of succeeding generations.

Out of the depths of the past and of early New England rise the names of John Winthrop, Governor of Massachusetts; Miles Standish, the warrior Pilgrim of the Mayflower; Peregrine White, the first Pilgrim child; John Elliott, the Pilgrim minister; John Mason, the Indian warrior; Thomas Hooker, the light of the Western Churches; and Roger Williams, who was banished from

Massachusetts, only to erect a more perfect altar of freedom within the boundaries of Rhode Island and Providence.

Thus it will be seen that the founders of the Commonwealth, comprising the people of New England, were Englishmen. While the emigration to New England began in 1620, it was not large, until 1630, and in 1640 it had nearly ceased. These New England people, consisting at that time of not more than twenty thousand persons, thenceforward multiplied on their own soil, in remarkable seclusion from other communities for nearly one and a half centuries. Some slight emigrations from it took place at an early day, but they were soon discontinued, and it was not until the last quarter of the 18th century that those swarms began to depart from New England, which have since occupied so vast a portion of the United States. During this long period the identity of New Englanders remained unimpaired. No race was ever more homogeneous down to half a century ago. It is said that the millions of living persons, either born in New England, or tracing their origin to the natives of that region, are descendants of those twenty thousand Englishmen who came over to New England before the early emigration ceased, upon the meeting of the long Parliament. The Cromwellian Scotch prisoners at Boston can scarcely be traced. A few families of French Huguenots in Massachusetts; a few Scotch-Irish families in New Hampshire, constitute the main exceptions.

Thus the people of New England, until the last half century, were a singularly unmixed race. No county in England can furnish purer English blood. The Pilgrim Fathers also represented a peculiar type of the Englishmen of the 17th century. A very large majority were Puritans. Occasionally there were other elements, but a substantial conformity to the Puritan standard became universal. Thus this people, aloof from foreign influence for one and a half centuries, was forming its own character, creating its own discipline and solving its own problems.

Until the war of 1775, New England knew but little of the commonwealths which finally engaged with her in that conflict. Until then, Massachusetts and Virginia, the two principal English Colonies, had no mutual ties; no common action, and but few relations either of business or acquaintance.

New Englanders in those early days had distinct and positive characteristics. They were a prolific race. They married early in life and married often if opportunity occurred. They always rejoiced to have their homes "edified and beautified with many children."

They were emphatically a thinking community. Their strong traits of character were not of the hand, the pocket or the heart, but of the brain. New England was filled with graduates of the great English universities of Cambridge and Oxford. Especially were their clergy, men not merely of deep piety, but scholars of eminent learning.

In their log houses, with the howling of the wolves ringing in their ears, they read the Hebrew Bible and the classic authors of Greece and Rome. They were a thoroughly intellectual people. Yet religion was still the one supreme thing in life, and towards this end their efforts were all directed.

It was a life of severity and rigid discipline even to asceticism, and from it some dark shadows fall.

To-day we smile when we read that an aged and devout female saint expressed deep horror that a whalebone should be worn in the bodice, and that a certain godly man had his band "something stiffened with starch;" that the smoke of tobacco was compared to the smoke ascending from the bottomless pit; that grave divines thundered against long hair, and that statesmen in solemn conclave counseled how they might crop the heads of the multitude.

They could not tolerate an unbeliever. They were divided into closely related communities that were possessed of local self-government. No one, unless a member of the church, was allowed a voice in the State. Every man was educated. Labor was regarded as honorable; idleness as disgraceful. Their minds and consciences were constantly at work. Thus under no warm, mellow sky, but upon the bleak New England coast they worked out their own society and their own development.

In physical and spiritual stock the people of New England were well started, and of such a race under such circumstances, any result however unparalleled, might well be predicted. They each rejoiced in what they believed to be the glory of God's intervention in aiding them in their work of erecting a great religious commonwealth in America.

Their emigration to the New World was a sacred and not a secular act. They were soldiers of Christ, doing battle under his banners and looking for their reward beyond the clouds. Such were some of the most important circumstances attending the development of early New England life.

We have spoken of their first years of distress. They were soon followed by seasons of abundance and happiness. A nation had been planted! A commonwealth matured! Plenty soon prevailed. The people were full of affection and their objects of love were around them. They enjoyed religion. They were ever industrious, enterprising and frugal. Affluence naturally followed these conditions of life. The duration of life increased, and the purity of their morals made the picture of colonial felicity almost without a blemish.

In 1643 fifty towns and villages dotted the landscape of the New World. One million of dollars had been expended in settling and developing this. People, manufactures, commerce and the arts were rapidly introduced. Over 300 emigrant ships had anchored in Massachusetts Bay. Over twenty thousand people had found an asylum.

These circumstances paved the way for the creation of an incipient Union! A political organization was formed, embracing Massachusetts, Plymouth, Connecticut and New Haven, called " The United Colonies of New England," a confederacy which lasted nearly half a century.

Thus did New England take the foremost step in political science and create a government of the most unmixed simplicity.

We cannot here follow New England in her chronological development. We all know how gallantly she acted her part in the severe conflicts between the aggressions of the mother country and the independence of the colonies of America.

It was Massachusetts who in 1664, bravely and successfully repelled the bold attempt of Charles the Second to control the New England Colonies, and who sent back to England in humiliation her Royal Commissioners who landed at Boston, intending to subvert the colonial liberties.

In King Philip's war many of the pride and flower of New England fell upon the field; but with the death of this Indian warrior in 1676, the Indian race was swept from New England.

We are all familiar with the futile attempt of James the Second in 1686, to revoke the Colonial Charters, and how in that hour of dangerous invasion, it seemed as if the liberties of New England were departing forever.

How Massachusetts lay prostrate at the feet of this English despot. How Joseph Wadsworth snatched the Charter of Connecticut and concealed it in the hollow of the Charter Oak! And how before the Summer of 1688 had gone, the undying spirit of New England Independence asserted itself, shining with meridian power, and the former liberties of New England were *regained* and placed upon a permanent foundation. How Massachusetts in 1690, gloriously came to the rescue of her mother country in her war with France, and uttered in aid thereof, the first American paper money! How all New England joined hands in those several fierce conflicts which finally resulted in the overthrow of French power in America.

As we approach the period of the American Revolution, New England shines forth as the brilliant, glittering, guiding star of American Liberty. Massachusetts alone had within her borders two hundred thousand souls of European ancestry, among whom the principles of Puritanism held universal sway. Her system of free schools caused New England to lead in the cause of education. Within her borders prior to the Revolution, so universal were her means of education, that there was not to be found in all New England an adult who could not read and write. Already the Colleges of Harvard, William and Mary, Princeton, Dartmouth and Yale were busy educating the people of New England.

We need not be surprised that when the storm of the Revolution burst with its terrible earnestness and fury, New England was ready for the conflict. Not indeed in "men of war" or disciplined soldiery or approved weapons of modern warfare, but equipped with that material of heart and brain and principle from which springs forth a race of soldiers and an army of men, who may die, but will never surrender.

It was James Otis, of Massachusetts, "that flame of fire" as he was called by John Adams, who presided at the birth and baptism of American Independence. It was his speech before the General Court of Massachusetts against English Writs of Assistance, that insured National Freedom.

Samuel Adams and the "Boston Tea Party," adorn the pages of New England history. The Boston Port Bill inaugurated the American Revolution. Concord, Lexington and Bunker Hill are Mecca's for the freedom-loving pilgrims of the world.

We cannot say that there is no fleck or dark spot upon the horizon of New England which the ardent historian would not fain obliterate. Humanity even in its most exalted forms may hardly aspire to absolute perfection.

The picture of Massachusetts would not be accurate without the blemish of the witchcraft of Salem. The same town that banished Roger Williams, at a later day became the scene of the most fatal delusion of modern times. Yet the faults and imperfections of New England may well be forgotten in the dazzling glory of her achievements.

In the silent but onward march of human progress, she has always been in the van. Her incomparable line of soldiers, patriots, scholars, jurists, divines and statesmen attest her perfect development. In the thickest of the battle, the flags of New England were ever to be seen. In the darkest hour of National peril she became an impregnable tower of strength.

When the dangerous heresy of State Rights in 1830, threatened to dissever the Union; when the glittering theories of Southern aggression paled the faces of our patriot statesmen, and the Union seemed rocking in uncertainty, it was New England's unrivaled master of American oratory, Daniel Webster, of Massachusetts, that fearless expounder of the nation's Constitution, who arose in the Senate of the United States, and with his irresistible and unanswerable logic and argumentation overwhelmed in dismay the brilliant advocates of Disunion.

New England has long been the center of American power. When once her gates opened to emigration, her principles spread rapidly to the neighboring States, and finally imbued the whole continent. Her influence and her greatness have long since ceased to be measured by her geographical boundaries. From the rocky shores of the Atlantic to the golden slopes of the Pacific, go where you will, and you shall feel and appreciate the influence of New England in American civilization. What department of human knowledge has she not explored? What storehouses of religious, literary, political and scientific wealth she has securely garnered. What land opened to the lessons of the 19th century, has not heard her voice? Who can doubt that in our last great struggle for national life, New England was the controlling vital factor in the full regeneration of the American Republic?

New England has expanded beyond the boundaries of this Western Hemisphere. She is no longer the rebellious subject of Old England. Conscious of her superiority she challenges the admiration and the competition of all Europe.

The Pilgrim Fathers of the 17th century sleep in honored graves. As the years roll on, more heroic seem their labors; more radiant their glory; and more plainly is revealed the hand of God in their history.

We, the descendants of New England, are proud of our

ancestry. We revere their memory and cherish their traditions. Our hearts go out to them in unmeasured gratitude. "They builded better than they knew."

An impenetrable veil conceals the future of our country. It is wrapped in the mysteries of God.

Not long since, in the city of New York, the mournful requiem, and the funereal dirge commemorated the last scene in the busy life of one of New England's most gifted sons, that patriarch of journalism and the earliest of America's most famous poets, William Cullen Bryant. Silvered with the snows of more than eighty winters he departed; transmitting to us the example of a pure and ennobled life; a New England character of the highest type; unsullied with the taints of worldly temptations and unmarred by the heels of time. More than half a century ago, while yet a student in New England's classic halls, he laid down this immortal rule of life, which like virtue, has furnished its own best reward, and won for him an imperishable fame.

It shall be the benediction which I invoke upon the descendants of New England.

> "So live, that when thy summons comes to join
> The innumerable caravan that moves
> To the pale realms of shade, where each shall take
> His chamber in the silent halls of death,
> Thou go not, like the quarry-slave at night,
> Scourged to his dungeon, but, sustained and soothed
> By an unfaltering trust, approach thy grave
> Like one who wraps the drapery of his couch
> About him, and lies down to pleasant dreams."

E. D. K.

THE MILITARY TRACT.

In the early settlement of several counties of Central New York, the "Military Tract" had a conspicuous part, and a sketch of its history will have considerable interest at this time when the facts are less familiar than they were half a century ago. The settlement of titles and the gradual subdivision of these lands have obliterated the distinctive lines which for a time kept fresh the boundaries and divisions of the "Military Tract," but nevertheless whoever now undertakes to search out the claims of ownership to property in that great "Tract," will speedily discover the importance of a familiarity with the history of it. The facts connected with the creation, laying out and distribution of these lands are briefly as follows :—

On the 16th of September, 1776, the Congress of the United States passed a resolution giving bounty lands to officers, non-commissioned officers and privates, serving in the Continental army. The last two named parties to receive each one hundred acres. The officers bearing commissions to receive from one hundred and fifty to five hundred acres each. By a resolution passed August 12, 1780, it was declared a Major-General should receive eleven hundred acres of land.

In 1783, March 27th, the Legislature of the State of New York

Resolved, "That this State is willing not only to take upon themselves to discharge the engagements thus made by Congress, so far as it relates to the line of this State, but likewise, as a gratuity to said line ; and to evince the just sense this Legislature entertains of the patriotism and virtue of the troops of this State, serving in the army of the United States, it is ordered that besides the bounty land so promised by Congress this Legislature will by law provide that the Major-Generals and Brigadier-Generals now serving in the line of the army of the United States, and being citizens of this State; and the officers and privates of regiments of infantry commanded by Colonels Van Schaick and Van Cortland, and of the artillery commanded by Colonel Lamb, and of the corps of sappers and miners, as were when they entered the service inhabitants of this State, together with others, herein mentioned, shall severally have granted to them the following quantities of land, to wit:—

To Major-Generals..........................5,500 acres.
To Brigadier-Generals......................4,250 "
To Colonels................................2,500 "
To Lieutenant-Colonels.....................2,250 "
To Majors..................................2,000
To Captains and Regimental Surgeons, each..1,500 "
To Chaplains...............................2,000 "
To Non-Commissioned Officers and Privates... 500 "

It was also

Resolved, "That the lands to be granted as *bounty* from the United States and as a *gratuity* from this State, shall be laid out in townships of six miles square, and into one hundred and fifty-six lots of one hundred and fifty acres each; two lots whereof shall be reserved for the use of ministers of the gospel, and two for the use of schools."

The location of these lands was fixed by resolution passed on the 25th of July, 1782, in the central portion of the State. The Legislature from time to time modified this act, until it was ordered May 11, 1784, that the townships to be surveyed should contain 60,000 acres of land, and one hundred lots of 600 acres each, and be laid out as nearly in squares as local circumstances will admit; and be numbered one progressively, to the last inclusive, and

"The Commissioners of the Land Office shall likewise designate every township by such name as they shall deem proper." By this act it was provided, that if any person should assign to the Surveyor-General of the State, for the use of the people of the State, their claim to lands to be assigned to them by act of Congress above referred to, they should receive a like number of acres of land to be located in this State and so far as possible, in one tract; if the amount did not exceed one-fourth of a township. April 6, 1790, it was ordered by the Legislature that the quantity of fifty acres in one of the corners of the lots to be laid out in squares of 600 acres, shall be subject to the payment of the sum of forty-eight shillings to the Surveyor-General, as a compensation in full for his services in surveying, mapping and numbering the lots. If this sum of forty-eight shillings remained unpaid two years after the issue of the patents, this fifty acres was to be sold at public vendue; and the money arising from the sale paid, to the amount of forty-eight shillings, to the Surveyor-General, and any surplus was to be used to defray the expenses of constructing roads in the tract. By act of 1789, six lots in each township were reserved, one for the promotion of the gospel, one for public schools, one to promote literature, and the remaining to satisfy any claim arising by a person's drawing lots, the greater part of which was covered by water. The act of 1780 provided that if the soldiers who were to receive one hundred acres or more from the United States, failed to relinquish their claims to the State, then the Commissioners were to reserve for the use of the people of the State one hundred acres in each lot to which such person was entitled. This gave rise to the term "State's Hundred," so frequently applied to sections of land on the "Military Tract."

The Land Commissioners consisted of the Governor, Lieutenant-Governor, Speaker of the Assembly, Secretary of State, Attorney-General and the Treasurer, and Auditor of the Canal Department, the presence of three being necessary to form a quorum. At a meeting of this Commission, held at the Secretary's office in the city of New York, on Saturday, 3d of July, 1790, there were present, his excellency George Clinton, Governor, Lewis A. Scott, Secretary, Gerard Bancker, Treasurer, and Peter T. Curtenius, Auditor.

"The Treasurer laid before the Board maps of the survey of twenty-five townships made by the Surveyor-General, Simeon DeWitt, on each of which maps the said townships respectively were subdivided into one hundred lots, containing six hundred acres each; whereupon the Board caused the townships and lots therein to be numbered according to law, and designated them by the names they now bear, to-wit: Lysander, Hannibal, Cato, Brutus, Camillus, Manlius, Cicero, Pompey," &c. (How much Simeon DeWitt had to do with the naming of the towns does not appear, although he is generally credited with this nomenclature). The claims of persons entitled by law to lands were presented; and Robert Harper and Lewis A. Scott were appointed to draw by ballot, as had previously been provided by act of Legislature, the lots of land to which they were entitled. These twenty-five townships constituted at the time, the "Military Tract," embracing the present counties of Onondaga, Cayuga, Cortland, Seneca, part of Tompkins and part of Oswego, except certain reserves for the Onondaga and Seneca Indians, and for the State of New York in the vicinity of the Salt Springs. Surveyor-General DeWitt personally laid out the "Military Tract," by plotting and mapping the boundaries and calculating the whole area. He was assisted in his field duties by several competent subordinates. Under this division towns and townships were frequently confounded; a town often embraced several townships. As settlements increased, some of the towns were subdivided. The whole "Tract" originally contained about one million eight hundred thousand acres, or about three thousand rights, exclusive of reservations. The Indian titles were extinguished by the treaty of Fort Stanwix, September 12, 1788.

Letters-patent were afterwards issued to the proper claimants, signed by the Governor and Secretary of State, to which were affixed the great seal of the State. These letters patent reserved to the State "all gold and silver mines, and also five acres of every one hundred, for highways." If, within the term of seven years, there was not one actual settlement made on the lot of land granted, the same reverted to the State.

The soldiers who were entitled to these lands, in nearly every instance sold their claim; and frequently more than once. The consideration received was often very small. Speculators who purchased these titles afterwards sold to the settlers. No place for recording deeds being available, the same lands were not unfrequently purchased from parties who had not the first title, and settlers found themselves in possession of conflicting titles, and in some instances, without any just claims whatever. To adjust these opposing interests, the Legislature, about the year 1795, appointed a commission, who from the best information gained, awarded the titles to the proper parties. Until this commission was appointed and had performed its work, the "Military Tract" did not rapidly become settled. Settlers preferred to preempt land, or to settle upon lands whose titles were more to be relied upon.

In illustrating the evil which grew out of the repeated sales of these lands and the confusion of ownership, we cite the case of Mr. Joseph Shattuck, who purchased a title to a lot of land in the town of Pompey, settled upon it with nine sons, men grown; he cleared sixty acres, built a log house and a log barn, when, to his surprise, he learned that the lot properly belonged to Conrad Bush, who through legal process ejected him from the premises. He then bought a farm near this one, and having made some improvements upon it was forced to leave it to others. He then declared he would not remain upon the "Military Tract," and, with six sons, he went west, to the town of Cohocton, Genesee county, and there made a permanent settlement. These experiences will apply in the case of many of the early settlers and improvers of these lands, but long since all the elements of confusion and conflicting titles were extinguished, and to very few of the present peaceful occupants of these lands are the facts of the early history of them known. Little, indeed, do we of to-day appreciate the trials and difficulties of those who laid the foundation of our present prosperity.

GENEALOGICAL RECORD.

Tracing our ancestral line, reaching two hundred and fifty years or more into the past, we are able in the light of reliable records, to follow Henry Kinne, born in 1624, from Holland to Salem, Mass., where he settled on a farm in 1653. It is believed that he was born in Norfolk, England, where his father, Sir Thomas Kinne, lived, having been knighted by the government for some signal service rendered it; and that following the tide of emigration through Holland, where they sought greater religious liberty, but found less than the fullest freedom, Henry came to Salem at about thirty years of age. He was a prosperous farmer, and was employed to some extent in ecclesiastical work.

His children were eight in number, three sons and five daughters. His second son, Thomas, from whom our branch springs, was born in 1656, and in 1677 was married to Elizabeth Knight, by whom he had four sons, of whom Thomas the oldest, and who is in our line, removed to Preston, now Griswold, Conn., in 1715, at the age of thirty-seven. When this Thomas the 2d sold out in Salem, he signed his name *Kinne* to a deed, and carried this spelling of the name to Connecticut with him, and his gravestone now stands on the banks of the Tackany river, in Griswold, bearing this same form which the Kinnes still use, at least the Onondaga county branch.

Thomas Kinne had ten sons and six daughters born to him from 1702 to 1727. His oldest son, Jeremiah, who died in Voluntown, Conn., married Mary Starkweather, and had thirteen children, of whom the fifth, a son, David, married Eunice Cogswell, by whom twelve children were born to him. The eighth, a daughter, Elizabeth, was the mother of eleven children, of whom the writer, Emerson Kinne, is the second. The sixth son of Thomas Kinne was Moses, who died in Voluntown, Conn. He also had a numerous family of whom Cyrus was one, and the one in our line.

His third son, Prentiss Kinne, was the father of the writer.

Having thus traced our lineage, recapitulated and abridged, it stands thus:

Born.		Died.
1624, Henry Kenney,	Salem,	1712
1656, Thomas Kenney,	"	1687
1678, Thomas Kinne,	Preston,	1756

Born.	Died.	Born.	Died.
1710, Moses Kinne,	1788	1702, Jeremiah Kinne,	1798
1746, Cyrus Kinne,	1808	1736, David Kinne,	1808
1773, Prentiss Kinne,	1830	1774, Elizabeth Kinne,	1820

HISTORY OF CYRUS KINNE.

Cyrus Kinne, the progenitor of the Kinne family of this County of Onondaga, was born in Voluntown, Windham County, State of Connecticut, Aug 11, 1746. As stated above he was one of a numerous family of brothers, four of whom were on the tented fields of the Revolution.

Cyrus Kinne married Comfort Palmer, of Voluntown, in the year 1768, and resided there until the year 1779, when he removed to the township of Petersburgh, Rensselaer County, State of New York, on land then known as the Van Rensselaer estate.

In the year 1791, while on business in the city of Troy, where the Surveyor General, Simeon DeWitt, was holding a public sale of some State lands lying in what is now the County of Onondaga, he became sufficiently interested, to look over the map where these lands were represented as lying. Noticing the numerous streams running through these lands, he was induced to bid on some of the survey fifties. As a consequence several of these lots, lying in what is now the town of Manlius, were struck off to him. Returning home he told his family what he had done, and so soon as he could arrange his business he started on horseback to view the country where some of this land lay. At this time, there were but few inhabitants west of Utica, and west of Oneida there were no roads, only Indian trails. He came, looked over the land he had purchased, and found some of it to be good for farming land, and some to be low and swampy, but was so well pleased with the general appearance of the country, that he bought more land lying near that already purchased.

Returning home he sold his leased land which he held on the Patroon's Manor, closed up his business, and in the month of March, 1792, started with an ox-team before a sled, and one horse, accompanied by his four oldest sons, namely, Ezra, Zachariah, Prentiss and Ethel.

West of Oneida they were obliged to cut their own roads. The writer of this sketch has often heard one of the number relate incidents that occurred during the journey.

There being no bridges they crossed the streams as best they could, sometimes unloading the heavy articles and carrying them over the streams on fallen trees and reloading them.

They came through this new and wild country to where Fayetteville now is, about the first of April, and settled on some of the land he had bought, built a log house, cleared some land and planted corn and potatoes.

In the month of June he returned to bring the remaining part of his family to his new home. From the time he left, in June, until his return, in July, the four boys above named that were left in the new home in the forest, had by turns to be their own housekeepers, and they have often been heard to say, that it seemed very pleasant to have their mother occupying her accustomed place at the table with them.

The nearest grist-mill was at Oneida, but grist-mills, as

well as saw-mills, were soon erected and put in order for use.

Cyrus Kinne was a mechanic as well as a farmer. He brought with him a set of blacksmith tools with which he did the first blacksmith work that was done in the town of Manlius.

Land was rapidly cleared and brought under cultivation, wheat and corn were soon grown in quantities sufficient for home consumption.

Albany was the nearest market for their surplus of produce, and it soon became the business of the more able farmers to carry their surplus produce on sleighs to Albany in the winter, as the roads in summer were almost impassable. Fish and wild game were very plenty. Limestone Creek, running through some of the land that Mr. Kinne had bought and occupied, was well stocked with salmon. They were easily taken, so easily that they were sometimes caught with pitchforks.

The father of the writer has often been heard to say, that he caught seven large ones in an afternoon. Bears and wolves were troublesome, so that sheep had to be folded at night. Pigs and even small hogs were often taken out of the pen and carried off. But this state of things did not long continue, as settlements thickened and inroads were made into these forests the wild animals became shy and receded before the march of the sturdy settlers.

The father of these stalwart boys, mindful of their coming wants, as they might desire to settle in homes of their own and rear families, had made his own, by ample purchases, sufficient quantities of land to give each, one hundred acres.

His three oldest, *Ezra*, *Zachariah* and *Prentiss* he settled in the town of Manlius, now DeWitt. His fourth son, *Ethel*, settled in Manlius, but he soon sold his one hundred acres and settled in the town of Cicero. *Zebulon* and *Moses*, twins, were settled in the town of Locke, Cayuga County, but the location not suiting them the land was sold, and they settled in the town of Cicero. This town has since been divided, and one of the hundred acres lies in the town of Clay. His seventh son, *Joshua*, also settled in the town of Cicero. His eighth son, *Cyrus*, was settled in Manlius. His ninth son, *Japheth* was settled in what is now the town of Clay, on a hundred acres adjoining that of his brother Moses. His tenth son, *Palmer*, was not of age at the death of his father, but was provided by will with a farm in the town of Cicero.

The oldest daughter, *Rachel*, was married to William Williams, and settled in the town of Manlius.

The youngest daughter, *Comfort*, married Jerry Springsted, and settled in the town of Cicero.

Cyrus Kinne, Esq., died Aug. 8th, 1808, at the age of sixty-two years. He left a large farm lying on the north side of the road running through the village of Fayetteville, to be sold and the avails of the same to be divided among his children.

The first inhabitants of the town of Manlius, were chiefly from New England. Some few families located in different parts of the town, from 1790 to 1793; but it was not till 1794, the date of the organization of the county, that Manlius was much known abroad. In that year settlers began to look towards it as a desirable place to locate as a residence.

The first town-meeting was held at the tavern of *Benjamin Morehouse*, April 1st, 1794. *Cyrus Kinne* was chosen Chairman, and Levi Jerome Secretary of this meeting.

In every sphere in which *Mr. Kinne* was called to act,

he was an active and energetic man. In looking over the minutes of the Baptist Church at Fayetteville, we notice that *Cyrus Kinne* was one of the most prominent persons in the organization of that church of that place, then known as Manlius Four Corners.

Cyrus Kinne and Gersham Breed came to this place in 1792, and were soon followed by *Daniel Campbell.* These three, in company with Mrs. Susanna Ward, formed themselves into a conference for religious worship, maintaining covenant meetings and enjoying occasional preaching.

In 1798 three young men were added to the conference, which was soon still further augmented by other Christian families who had moved into the neighborhood. Their first meetings were of necessity held in private dwellings, but for many years afterwards were held in the wood and stone school houses. In 1804, a council was called, at which Father Bennett and Elder John Peck were present, and this company of brethren and sisters, in number about twenty, were recognized as a regular and independent church. In attendance at this meeting, we notice the names of some of them. Cyrus Kinne, Gersham Breed, Daniel Campbell, Jabez York, Lewis Sweeting, John Jones, Zopher Knowlton, Orris Hopkins, William Breed, Allen Breed, Palmer Breed, Washington Worden, Susanna Ward, Mary Terrill, Amelia Breed, Hannah Breed, Lucretia Worden, Mrs. Kinne, Elizabeth Hopkins and Walter Worden. Brother Gersham Breed was licensed as preacher. In 1812 he was ordained and became the first pastor of the church.

Mr. Kinne was notably identified with the early history of the county, was one of the first Justices of the Peace in the county, and tradition says he married the first couple that were married in the town of Manlius.

Nearly all of his children reared large families.

Ezra, his eldest son, married Mary Young; there were born to them twelve children.

Zachariah, the second son, married Diadama Barnes; to them ten children were born.

Prentice Kinne, the third son, married Elizabeth Kinne, a distant relative; eleven children were born to them.

Ethel, the fourth son, married a Miss Eaton; five children were born to them—four sons and one daughter.

Zebulon, the fifth son, married Lucy Markham, by whom he had eight children.

Moses, the sixth son, married Betsey Williams; these reared eight children.

Joshua, the seventh son, married a Miss Leach; they reared eight children.

Cyrus, the eighth son, married Asenith Warner; they reared four children.

Japheth, the ninth son, married Temperance Palmer; they reared four children.

Palmer, the tenth son, married Polly Carr; they reared six children.

Rachel, the elder of the two daughters, married William Williams; they reared four children.

Comfort, the younger daughter, married Jerry Springsted; they reared six children.

The above shows Cyrus Kinne to have had eighty-six grandchildren arrive at maturity.

FAMILY OF PRENTICE KINNE.

As shown above, the grandfathers of *Prentice Kinne* and *Elizabeth Kinne* were brothers, and hence their fathers were cousins.

They were married January 16th, 1800, at the home of her father, in the town of Plainfield, Connecticut. In the spring of 1800 they commenced housekeeping on the farm where they lived the remainder of their lives.

Mr. Kinne has often been heard to say that he was the first white man that ever struck a blow on his hundred acres, unless it was done by a surveyor.

The farm was cleared and made very productive, and became the home of a large and happy family.

Julius C., the oldest son, was born October 19th, 1802.

He and Mrs. Rachel Willard were married October, 1831. They had five children, four sons and a daughter; two of the sons died in childhood.

Emerson, the second son, was born February 16th, 1804.

He and Miss Janet Luddington were married May 23rd, 1833. They have no living children.

Marvin, the third son, born March 4th, 1806, died February 23rd, 1813.

Eunice, the oldest daughter, was born October 22nd, 1807, and was married to Wesley Bailey, August 23rd, 1833. There were born to them six children, three of whom died in childhood.

Mason Prentice, the fourth son, born November 30th, 1808, was married to Mary Jane Spaulding, 1840. They had five children, two of them died in childhood.

Elbridge, the fifth son, was born May 26th, 1810.

He married Sophionia Young, October 17th, 1837. There were born to them six children—three sons and three daughters; one son and one daughter died young.

N. Hildreth, the sixth son, was born March 20th, 1812, and married Diantha Kinne.

There were born to them four children—three sons and a daughter; one son and the daughter died in infancy.

Their son, *Eugene*, lived to manhood.

Emily, the second daughter, born December 4th, 1813, married Curran Elms, and had seven children—four sons and three daughters.

Salome, third daughter, born May 8th, 1815, married Dewitt C. Peck, October 29th, 1840, and had seven children, six sons and a daughter. Two sons died in childhood.

Atlas, the seventh son, born May 27th, 1817, and married Renette Palmer, May 8, 1839. He died March 15th, 1845.

Ansel, the eighth son, born May 17th, 1820, married Emma Merrick, October 16, 1849. There were born to them seven children, three sons and four daughters; one son and one daughter died in childhood.

George N., the ninth son, and by the second marriage, was born January 24th, 1829.

There are now, March 13, 1879, thirty-one living children of the second generation of Prentice Kinne.

Having thus briefly traversed the line of our ancestry through seven generations, it is deemed desirable and proper, to pause and review, giving more extended notes, from personal knowledge and observation, of the histories and incidents connected with the family of our parents, *Prentice* and *Elizabeth Kinne*, of revered and blessed memory!

As one that knew Prentice Kinne better, and recollects more of him than any other person now living, I deem it not out of place to commit some of these recollections to paper.

My earliest remembrance of my father was at the burial

of my grandfather, Cyrus Kinne, in the year 1808, when I was four years old.

I very clearly recall seeing my father with three of his brothers act as bearers, taking up the coffin at the house and lowering it into the grave. Some years later I learned that this was done at the request of grandfather, something very unusual at this late day.

A few years later, in 1812, I remember seeing him when he commanded a train band, and a little later when he was second in command of a regiment during the war. He had no difficulty in gaining and holding the attention of his command. In illustration of this fact, I will here relate an incident that occurred during the war of 1812 and 1815. At one time the British effected a landing at Oswego, took possession of the garrison, drove our force out of the place and destroyed the government property. The country became alarmed. The military of Onondaga County was called out and ordered to repair to Oswego as soon as possible. The regiment was commanded by Col. Thaddeus M. Wood. A short time previous to this, my father had been promoted from a captaincy to the second in command of the regiment. His commission had been forwarded to the County Clerk's office, then at Onondaga Hollow, but he had not taken it from the office, consequently was not in command. But he resolved to go as a private. He set my older brother and myself to molding bullets, which he put into a bag, and the powder into a flask, shouldered his firelock and started for Salt Point, as it was then called, the regiment having been ordered to rendezvous at this place, thence to proceed to Oswego. Col. Wood seeing my father without his uniform, remonstrated with him for so appearing. Father replied that he was not in commission, to which Col. Wood said " You are not going in this way.

You send home for your uniform and I will send to the Clerk's office for your commission. It was so arranged. The troops were placed on board boats. There being but little wind the boats had to be propelled mostly by oars, hence but slow progress made. The men at the oars complained and wished to be relieved. The soldiers refused to assist, saying their work was to fight, not to row boats. Father seeing the situation, and being in command on that boat, arose, drew his sword and addressed them thus:— "Fellow Soldiers: This is no time to parley or hesitate. We are called upon to drive an invading enemy from our soil. They have gained a foothold. We know not but they may be now burning and pillaging the homes of our citizens. It is as much our business to get where they are, as to fight them when we are there. Let me not see a man refuse to take his turn at the oar. I am one with you and will take my turn." There was no more holding back; every man was ready to do his share.

In 1814 the services of the militia were again in requisition. Gen. Brown, then in command at Sackets Harbor, suspecting the design of the enemy to be, to attack that place by crossing over from Canada, a requisition was made by the Governor, and the military were called out. Col. Wood was first in command and Major Kinne second. The regiment was ordered to rendezvous at Manlius Village. Thence the regiment marched by way of Rome to Smith's Mills, a place some twelve or fourteen miles distant from Sackets Harbor. Here the regiment encamped and awaited orders. During the encampment, Col. Wood being ill, the command devolved upon Major Kinne. By this timely caution and preparation, the suspected attack was prevented, and after a month's service, the regiment was disbanded and returned by way of Oswego to their homes.

In military father was a strict disciplinarian, and this trait was prominent in the government of his family. A look or a tap with his finger was generally sufficient to command attention. The rod was sometimes used, but always reluctantly. I have often seen the tears course down his face before using it. He was always kind and loving, especially so to our excellent mother, always enjoining upon the children to be mindful of her wants and make her task as light as possible. He was looked upon by his neighbors as a model man, in his family. He had one fault, and who is without faults? I speak of this painfully and reluctantly, but kindly. He sometimes indulged in the use of ardent spirits. The habit was formed in times, when it was deemed proper for the best of men, to keep it in their side-boards, and offer it to their friends and guests. Moreover, social men were even more apt to form habits of excess in this respect, than others. So then we cast kindly the mantle of charity over this, more a misfortune than a fault.

Our mother, Elizabeth Kinne, was the daughter of David Kinne, of Plainfield, Windham County, Connecticut, who was the son of Jeremiah Kinne, who was the son of Thomas Kinne 2nd. Jeremiah was a brother of Moses Kinne, who was the father of Cyrus Kinne, our grandfather on father's side, which makes, as seen in the first part of this sketch, our grandfathers cousins.

In 1796, while my father was on a visit to his native place in Voluntown, Connecticut, he was invited to visit the family of David Kinne, of Plainfield, a distance of fifteen miles. There, for the first time, he saw Elizabeth, who in time became his wife. My father has often said to me that he journeyed to Connecticut five consecutive winters. In January, 1800, he was married, and in January,

1801, moved to Manlius, Onondaga County, N. Y., where they commenced housekeeping.

In October, 1802, their son Julius was born. Our mother inherited a strong constitution, possessed great powers of endurance, or she never could have stood the hardships and privations incident to a commencement of a married life in a wilderness home. I well recollect her in my childhood days. Patient and untiring in her devotion to her children, always pleasant, she never permitted to pass, unimproved, any good opportunity of inculcating the principles of truthfulness and love to each other. So soon as we were old enough to be made useful, there was work for hands to perform. We had tasks set for us by our father, when he was to be absent on buisness. Left alone, our work would sometimes become irksome, and we discouraged and often out of patience. Our mother always had a word of encouragement for us, sometimes saying we were getting along finely, and our task would soon be done, and father would be pleased with what we had done. I never heard a word drop from her lips, that ran counter to any order that our father had given us. If she thought he was too severe in his requirements of us, it never reached our ears. She always taught us to be obedient to every command he gave us. I remember on some occasions, when things were not pleasant, mother's saying, " When you see anything wrong in others, be sure to avoid it in yourselves."

Mother was born and reared in a Christian family, but never made a public profession of religion, yet she inculcated the principles of Christianity in the minds of her children, by both example and precept, always prized good conduct above riches, and has often been heard to say that it was her prayer, that none of her children be rich, nor did she want to see them poor, but never above the necessity of laboring with their hands for their bread. She died November 5th, 1820 in the forty-seventh year of her age, of cancer in the breast, leaving ten children, the youngest, Ansel, only five months old. *Love and peace to her memory!*

In 1821 father married Eunice Jones of Madison County, formerly a resident of Preston, Windham County, Connecticut. In January, 1829, a son was born to them, George N. Kinne.

Father died July 19, 1830, in the fifty-seventh year of his age. Our stepmother was a good woman and a good mother to us all, and I have reason to believe that she was a Christian. She died October 22, 1858.

FAMILY OF JULIUS C. KINNE.

Julius C. Kinne, the oldest son of Prentice Kinne, as noted above, was born Oct. 19th, 1802.

Inheriting a strong constitution, having early acquired habits of industry, and possessing an intuitive perception of right and duty, he soon became the natural reliance of his parents for their young and numerous family. Owing to this fact, and the meagre facility for acquiring an education seventy years ago, he was able to obtain a knowledge of only the elements of an English education.

On the death of his father, which occurred at an early period of his majority, the responsibility of directing affairs of a large family of brothers and sisters devolved upon him, a responsibility which he discharged with such signal fidelity that the young members came to regard him with mingled feelings of paternal and fraternal affection.

Thoroughness and perseverance were the characteristics

which marked every transaction of his life. His home, his grounds and every feature of his farm bore evidence of this. Nor were his business relations with the community in which he lived less marked by these traits. Whatever project or enterprise engaged his time or attention engaged the whole of it, and no honorable means were left untried until success had crowned his efforts.

He was a close observer of the political movements of his time and often an active participant in their strifes. Elected to the Legislature of 1845 and again to that of 1846, his habits of industry and perseverance did not desert him there, but were available in the discharge of the various legislative duties to which he devoted his whole energies. His firm and consistent course while here fully met the views of his constituents and won the confidence of Governor Wright—a confidence which he ever appreciated and never betrayed. With the interest of the community in which he had always lived he was emphatically identified. Upright in character, sound in judgment, his advice was often sought. Strong in his sympathies he was the friend of the indigent and afflicted. None such ever turned from his door unrelieved where relief was possible.

Skilled in the appliances of means to an end and generous to a fault, his assistance was often solicited by those in perplexed circumstances, and many in the community held him in grateful remembrance for such assisstance.

But he rests from his labors, having died as he lived, with a firm confidence in a just, merciful and immutable Providence.

His death occurred August 5th, 1857. A widow and three children survive him. The widow now lives with her daughter, Mrs. Helen Williams, in Muskegon, State of Michigan.

Howard A., the oldest son, married Hannah Tobin and moved to the State of Iowa in 1860, where he now resides. During the war of the Rebellion he enlisted in a regiment of cavalry that was raised in Iowa, and mustered into service, he went with the brigade commanded by General Sully of the regular army, into Dakota Territory, where he did service against the Indians and suffered untold hardships for three years, and at the close of the war was mustered out of the service with credit to himself as a soldier.

Edward D., the second son of Julius C. and Rachel Kinne, was born Feb. 9th, 1841, in DeWitt, Onondaga County. He attended the High School of Syracuse, graduated from Cazenovia Seminary, Michigan University, and for four years was in the Columbia Law School at Washington, D. C., and was admitted to the Supreme Court of that District.

In 1867 he moved to Ann Arbor, Michigan, was admitted to the bar and commenced the practice of law. In 1868 he was admitted to practice in the United States Court.

He has been Recorder and District Attorney, and was Mayor of the city of Ann Arbor in 1875 and re-elected in 1876.

In the year of 1867 he married Mary C. Hawkins, daughter of Judge Olney Hawkins, and has one son. Few young men have a finer record or brighter prospects.

EMERSON KINNE.

Emerson Kinne, the second son, was born Feb. 16th, 1804. By referring to the dates of birth of these two brothers, it will be seen that their ages differ only by sixteen months, so that they grew to their maturity somewhat as twins, in sympathy, in purpose, in plans and in enterprise. Both inheriting good constitutions, subjected to the same discipline, enduring similar hardships, privations and disadvantages, they came to be the twofold directors and stalwart leaders of the numerous family of growing boys and girls, at the time Julius and Emerson reached their majority. Meagre opportunities for an education coupled with the fact that they were the chief dependence of their parents for the support of the family, their education was similarly limited. This lack felt by him, Emerson never sought a civil office.

The first he ever held was that of commissioner of highways for 1832 in the old town of Manlius. Not in attendance at the caucus which nominated him, he was much surprised when informed of the fact. His associates were Reuben H. Bangs and Seth Spencer.

The ticket was elected, and re-elected in 1833, but ever after that he declined holding any office in the town. After the town was divided his residence was in the new town of De Witt, and in 1848, he was elected one of the assessors of the town. In 1851, he was nominated and elected Supervisor, but was not at the caucus that put him in nomination. He was elected over his opponent, Mr. Joseph Breed, an excellent and popular man, was re-elected, with very little opposition, and the third time with but *one* opposing vote. This closed all his civil services.

He was often called upon to act as guardian for minor children, and in settling differences between individuals. As executor, or administrator he settled the estates of several persons. Was appointed by the Chancellor, the general guardian of four of the minor children of the late Seth Young, namely, Maria, Cordelia, William and Louisa Young, with power to divide the real estate, and convey the same by title deed. He was appointed executor of the will of the late Atlas Kinne; also of the will of the late John I. Devoe, and administrator of the will of the late John Devoe. Appointed also administrator of the estate of the late Julius C. Kinne, and the guardian of his two sons, Howard and Edward, and again, administrator of the estate of the late George N. Kinne, and of the estate of the late Zebulon Kinne. Nearly all of these were settled to the entire satisfaction of the parties interested.

From a boy up he took an interest and pride in military affairs. It may be that this tendency was inherited or inspired from his father, who, it has been seen, served under several commissions previous to the war of 1812, and did some service in that war as second in command of a regiment at Smith's Mills, near Sackets Harbor, in 1814. In 1828 he was commissioned Ensign of a company of infantry by acting Governor Nathaniel Pitcher, and was elected Lieutenant in 1829, and Captain in 1830. In 1833 was elected Major, and in 1834 Lieutenant Colonel, and promoted to the command of the regiment in 1835. He was in command of this regiment for two years, and it was said to be the best disciplined regiment in the brigade. This compliment was bestowed by the commandant of the brigade. In 1837, he was commissioned Brigade Inspector of the Twenty-seventh Brigade of Infantry of the State of New York. As an officer he was pleasant and affable, though rigidly strict in discipline. It has been said of him, that his presence was commanding, his bearing dignified, his decisions generally just and his commands inexorable. Another said of him, "He is one of Nature's noblemen."

Politically, he was a Democrat, and during the Rebellion he was what was termed a war Democrat, sustaining the Government in crushing out the most causeless of rebellions, and nothing but his age prevented his taking an active part in it.

In 1833, he married Miss Janet Luddington. They have no living children. In 1831 he made a public profession of religion and united with the Baptist Church of Syracuse, where he has now a religious home. During that long period, he has labored in his humble way to promote the cause of Christ.

In 1831 he commenced taking the *Baptist Register*, then published in Utica, and has continued to do so through all of its changes up to the present time. The entire publication for fifty years, is still preserved and kept for the benefit of some person into whose hands it may fall.

Caution and care, prudence and push have characterized his life history, and this character has impressed itself upon many who have had personal knowledge of these characteristics. In short, his whole life has been an example of rare merit, challenging the admiration of all who knew him.

Marvin, the third son, was born March 4, 1806; was a very affectionate and kind-hearted boy, traits well remembered and appreciated by his older brothers. He did not inherit a strong constitution. His death, which occurred February 23, 1813, was his parents' first great grief, which was deeply shared in by the older brothers.

Eunice, the oldest daughter, born October 22nd, 1807, was a kind and dutiful daughter, laboring untiringly for the welfare of the younger members of the family. At the age of thirteen the death of her mother occurred, leaving her at this tender age, the oldest of eight children, the youngest a babe of five months. Heroic as was deemed the struggle of the older boys, mentioned before, it had its grand counterpart in this sister, who so well discharged the duties, and nobly met the responsibilities, now newly precipitated upon her. The babe of five months, now of threescore years, desires gratefully to record this tribute to his sainted sister's memory. To him, she was more than a sister. To her care and kindness, he, doubtless, owes his life, and this care and kindness never ceased while she lived.

She was united in marriage with Wesley Bailey, August 23rd, 1833. Mr. Bailey was all that a good husband and kind father could be to his family. His life was mainly spent in editing and publishing papers, especially in the interest of Anti-slavery and Temperance.

The *Liberty Press* and *Utica Teetotaller* were published in Utica, each for many years. See app.

There were born to Mr. and Mrs. Bailey six children, five sons and one daughter. Two sons died in childhood, the daughter, Janet, died at the age of seven years, and was a lovely little girl. Their oldest son, E. P. Bailey, was born Oct., 1834, at Manlius, New York. His early opportunity for an education was well improved. His father not having the means to give his son a college education, took him into his printing office at an early age in the city of Utica, there to learn the art of setting type. He soon found that there was work to be done at the desk with a pen, and preferring this to type-setting he was oftener found in the office than in the printing room.

Some twenty-five years ago, by the consent of his father, he left the office of the *Liberty Press* for the *Observer* office. The *Observer* was owned and published by Mr. Grove.

After working in that office for a number of years he bought an interest in the paper. It is now published by the firm of Grove & Bailey. For the last few years Mr. Grove has spent most of his time in New York, the business of the office being conducted almost entirely by Mr. Bailey.

50

As a political as well as a family paper it stands on a par with any paper in the State. It has a reputation as well as an influence second to none.

In September, 1857, he married Julia S. Wetherby, adopted daughter of *Emerson* and *Janet Kinne.* There was born to them a daughter, Feb. 1st, 1860. Mrs. Bailey's health soon failed, and July 9th, 1860, she died, leaving a sorrowing husband and a babe that never knew the care of a mother. In 1868 Mr. Bailey married Miss Hannah Chapman, of Utica.

There have been born to them four children, three sons and a daughter. The second, named Clinton, died in childhood. Two little boys and a darling little daughter are the light of their home. *Nettie*, their daughter, now twenty years old, is making herself useful in the loving care she has, for her little brothers and sister.

Ansel K., the second son of Eunice and Wesley Bailey, born 1835; received a fair education and went into his father's printing office with his older brother, E. P. Bailey, and there learned the art of printing as well as conducting a newspaper. In 1860 Mr. Wesley Bailey left Utica and moved to Decorah, Iowa, and there published the Decorah *Republican,* where it is continued by his two younger sons, Ansel K. and Alvan Stewart. In 1858 Ansel married Miss Sarah Higham, of Utica. There were born to them four children, three sons and one daughter, the latter was born in Utica Jan. 9th, 1860; their sons Edwin and Arthur K., were born in Decorah.

Ansel K. Bailey, County Treasurer for some time and Postmaster for several years, is regarded as a useful man in the community, is highly respected as upright in character and sound in judgement.

Alvan Stewart Bailey is with his brother Ansel in the publishing of the Decorah *Republican,* and both are prospering.

FAMILY OF MASON P. KINNE.

Mason P., fourth son of Prentice Kinne, was born in Manlius—now DeWitt, Nov. 30th, 1808. He received as good an education as the common schools of that early day afforded, and assisted his father on the farm until the death of the latter, when there was added to the old farm more land, and thus enlarged it was conducted by the five older brothers in the interest of the entire family.

This was continued for several years to the mutual satisfaction of all, and they were known and spoken of at home and abroad as the "Kinne boys."

The two older brothers, Julius and Emerson, having married, it was thought best to separate. Mason, Elbridge and Hildreth retaining the old farm, having already purchased the interest of all that had arrived at the age of twenty-one years, with the understanding that they were to secure the interest of all the minor heirs as they arrived at a proper age, so that the old farm might not be divided. This was accomplished amicably and satisfactorily.

The farming interest was conducted by these three brothers for several years.

On Jan. 30th, 1840, Mason P. married Mary Jane Spaulding, of Clarkson, Monroe County. There were born to them five children, four sons and a daughter. The daughter and a son died young, the daughter at about four years of age and the son, Ansel, at thirteen.

Charles Mason, their eldest son, born April 11th, 1841,

graduated from the Syracuse High School Jan. 1859, and immediately sailed for San Francisco, California, where he was employed in an agricultural warehouse until 1862, when, as a member of the "California Hundred," he came out with that body, equipped at their own expense, enlisted and sailed from San Francisco for Boston. Here the company tendered their services to Gov. Andrew and were mustered into service, being joined to the 2d Massachusetts Cavalry.

He was in over forty battles, and was once wounded. For his gallantry he was made Captain and Asst. Adj. Gen. of the Regular Brigade, First Cavalry Division under Gen. Gibbs. He was urged to remain in the regular army but he declared that the work for which he enlisted and volunteered was accomplished, viz: the Rebellion put down. He received an honorable discharge with a recommend for brevet Major for faithful service and meritorious conduct. He came home in July, 1865, and remained until the following spring when he returned to California with a wife and one child. They now have three children, one son and two daughters. Already, at the age of forty, his enterprise and push have won him a competence and an honorable standing in the community. (See app.)

Porter S., the second son, was a student in the High School of Syracuse; studied medicine, and is now practicing in Paterson, New Jersey. He married Amelia Smylie, of Paterson; they have two children.

Arthur, the third son, graduated from the High School of Syracuse; studied medicine as a profession and is now practicing in the city of Syracuse. He married Julia Smylie Oct. 14th, 1880.

Mason P. Kinne now resides on a part of the old farm. He has ever been an industrious business man, never seeking notoriety, but has been called to discharge the duties of several offices of the town, such as Assessor for ten years, Commissioner of Highways and Town Superintendent of Common Schools. Mr. Kinne always voted the Democratic ticket until 1853, since that time he has voted with the Republican party. He has exemplified the character of a consistent Christian.

FAMILY OF ELBRIDGE KINNE.

Elbridge, the fifth son, was born in Manlius, May 26th, 1810. Oct. 17th, 1837, he married Sophronia Young, daughter of Rev. Seth Young, of Dewitt, Onondaga county. There were born to them six children, three sons and three daughters. Their oldest, Theodore Y., was a graduate of the High School of Syracuse; studied medicine and commenced practice in Syracuse in the office of the late Dr. Clary. He volunteered as Asst. Surgeon in the Union army against the Rebellion; served in Virginia; went with his corps to Texas, and in July, 1865, received an honorable discharge. He returned home and the next spring commenced the practice of his profession again, and located in Paterson, New Jersey, where he now resides doing a prosperous business. He is not only a successful practitioner, but has large influence in the community where he resides. He was once chosen to read a paper before the Society of Homeopathists, of the State of New Jersey. He was again chosen to address the National Association at Philadelphia. In September, 1861, he married Ella Nottingham, of DeWitt. There were born to them three children, a son and two daughters.

Willie, oldest son of T.Y., was drowned while bathing in

the river, at the age of sixteen. He was a very promising and cultured young student.

Eliza, oldest daughter of Elbridge, was married to B. F. Barker, a young clergyman of the M. E. Church, June 4th, 1863. They have four children, three sons and a daughter.

Sophronia Janet, the second daughter of Elbridge, born September 15th, 1844, is a teacher of music, and a consistent Christian lady and dutiful daughter.

E. Olin, second son, now living, was a graduate of the High School of Syracuse, the University of the same place, and of the Medical College of Ann Arbor, Michigan. He is now practicing medicine in Syracuse, the eye and ear being a specialty with him. He is said to be a very thorough student.

Cornelia, a little daughter, died in childhood.

Albert, never a healthy child, died at the age of fifteen.

Elbridge Kinne, has ever resided on the old farm. Inheriting a strong constitution, he has ever been a laborious man, and in every place in farm work could lead where any could follow. Never ambitious for office, he has often been elected to fill some of the first offices of his town, as Supervisor, Justice of the Peace and Assessor for several years. In 1831 he made a public profession of religion and united with the Methodist Episcopal Church, where he has ever maintained a consistent, Christian character, and for over forty years has held official positions in the church and borne its burdens through all these years. He has been class-leader in the church for over forty years and clerk of the board of trustees of the same for forty-eight years, and been present at every meeting of the board except two, from which he was detained by personal sickness. Politically a Democrat, he has voted with the Republican party ever since its formation.

FAMILY OF N. HILDRETH KINNE.

N. Hildreth, the sixth son of *Prentice*, was born March 20th, 1812. At the age of twenty-one, was in company with his older brothers on a large farm for several years, and was prosperous in the business. During this time he was tendered the captaincy of a rifle company, attached to the 176th Regiment of Infantry, commanded by his brother Emerson. He was not a member of this company at this time, but accepted the offer, was elected and commissioned. He uniformed the company at his own expense; presented it with a beautiful stand of colors emblematical of the corps. The company soon attained a high rank in point of discipline, second to none in the regiment. He was assisted in this by his Lieutenant, D. C. Peck. About this time he severed his interest with his brothers, took his means and purchased a dairy farm in Oswego County, and remained there a few years, when, his health failing, he sold and came to the city of Syracuse to reside. He was elected one of the Colonels of the County. In 1860, his health having somewhat improved, he moved to Eaton County, Michigan, on to a small farm, where he now resides. In the the year 1840, March 9th, *N. H.* and *Diantha Kinne* were married. There were born to them four children, two dying in infancy.

Eugene, their oldest son, arrived at mature age, and was a faithful boy and a good scholar. He assisted his father on the farm in the summer seasons, and taught school in the winter. Never very robust, his health failed, and he died August 7th, 1877.

Emerson, their second son, is an excellent boy, has always been on the farm with his father, and is now his main reliance.

N. Hildreth made a public profession of religion in the

year 1832, and united with the Baptist Church of Syracuse, and has ever been a devoted Christian. He has suffered much from impaired health, and for the last five years, has been almost entirely confined to the house. There he is, prostrated and helpless, with little hope of ever mingling with the busy world and enjoying its activities, patiently waiting for the call to that rest promised to the faithful.

FAMILY OF EMILY KINNE.

Emily, the second daughter, born December 4th, 1813, was married to Mr. Curran Elms, a mechanic. They settled in Fayetteville. There were born to them seven children, four sons and three daughters. They moved from Fayetteville to VanBuren County, Michigan, and bought a small farm, on which father and sons labored until the Rebellion, when the two oldest sons, George and Byron enlisted, joined the army, were with Gen. Sherman on his great "march to the sea," and earned, each of them a commission. At the close of the war they were honorably discharged.

George is married and is living on a farm near Jackson, Michigan.

Byron is a mechanic and lives in Chicago.

Frederick, their third son is a salesman in a store for the sale of agricultural implements, in Charlotte, Michigan.

Jules, their fourth son, has recently graduated as a Homeopathic M. D., is married and has one child, a daughter. He is expecting to settle in the West as a practicing physician. More recently his brother, Byron, has graduated as a physician of the same school.

Lottie, their oldest daughter, married the Rev. Mr. Valentine, and lives in Grand Rapids, Michigan. Her two sisters, Lois and Florence live with her most of the time, are unmarried, Florence teaching in one of the schools of the same place.

Their mother, our sister *Emily*, died in the Spring of 1877. Mr. Elms is still living in Kalamazoo County, Michigan, at seventy years of age, hale and hearty.

FAMILY OF SALOME KINNE.

Salome, the third daughter of *Prentice* and *Elizabeth Kinne*, was born May 8th, 1815, and married DeWitt C. Peck, October 29th, 1840. There were born to them seven children, six sons and a daughter.

Herbert D. was born April 2nd, 1842. Attending the High School of Syracuse and the Cazenovia Seminary, he was in possession of a good education, when at the age of twenty-two he entered the United States Army as 2nd Lieutenant in Company E, New York Cavalry. He was mustered in at Rochester, N. Y., January 30th, 1864. After participating in several engagements in the Wilderness and at other points, on the march of Grant's army towards Petersburg, he was captured at Ream's Station, June 28th, 1864, while engaged in Wilson's raid on the Weldon and Petersburg Railroad. Lieut. Peck's prison life among the Rebels embraced limited periods, at Libby, Macon, Savannah, Charleston, Columbia and Wilmington prison, where he was paroled March 1st, 1865. Lee's surrender having canceled his parole, he came home on a furlough, remained a short time, then returned and joined his regiment. Soon after he received a Captain's commission, and remained in

Virginia on Provost duty until August, 1865, when his regiment was mustered out.

He was married to Amanda Burns, of Richmond, Ohio, and three children have been born to them. They now reside in Steubenville, Ohio. For some years he was engaged in a coal mine at Rush Run, now in mercantile trade.

Albert D., their second son, was born May 13th, 1846. Reared on the farm, educated in the district school, at the Syracuse High School, and at Cazenovia Seminary. He married Augusta Smull, of Columbus, Ohio, settled on a farm in Sac County, Iowa, was elected Recorder of that County, and is now in that public service making a record creditable to himself.

Clinton G., their third son now living, was born with a twin brother, Charles B., January 25th, 1852.

Charles died April 6th, 1858.

Edward S., born April 11th, 1849, died December 27th, 1857.

Clinton G. was reared and educated as were the brothers, graduated from the High School, Syracuse. Spent one summer on the farm in Iowa, with his brother Albert, came home the following winter, and has labored on the farm with his father, since. In June, 1878, he married Fannie Ferris of DeWitt. His health is impaired, and he and his wife spent the winter of '79 and '80 in the State of Iowa.

Willard H., the fourth living son of DeWitt and Salome Peck, born October 5th, 1854, educated as the brothers were, has spent his life thus far on the farm with his father, having taught school some in winters. He now resides in Iowa, engaged in the lumber trade.

Mary E., the only daughter, born February 15, 1856, is

well educated, a graduate from the High School, an excellent and dutiful daughter, residing at home.

DeWitt C. Peck and his wife Salome made a profession of religion before they were married, and united with the Methodist Episcopal Church, where they have led exemplary and devoted Christian lives, the influence of which has not been lost on their children, or the community in which they have lived.

Politically Mr. Peck was a Whig, casting his votes with that party until the organization of the Republican party, with which he has acted since. He has been elected to several offices of the town, but they have been imposed upon him, he never sought them.

FAMILY OF ATLAS KINNE.

Atlas, the seventh son of *Prentice* and *Elizabeth Kinne*, was born May 27th, 1817. He obtained a good common school education, and added thereto somewhat of an academic scholarship, and commenced teaching before his majority. Was on the farm with his brothers some after this, but most of his time was spent in teaching. At the age of twenty-two he was married to Renette Palmer of Fayetteville, Onondaga County, N. Y. There were no children born to them.

He was ambitious and energetic beyond his strength, and his constitution yielded under the excessive labor and exposure to which he was apt to subject himself. One who knew him well wrote, after his death, the following:

DIED.—In DeWitt, Saturday evening, March 15, 1845, of Consumption, Mr. Atlas Kinne, in the twenty-eighth year of his age.

The deceased was the son of the late Prentice Kinne Esq., and a member of a family of twelve children, ten of whom were living at the time of his death. He is the first of the number cut down in the vigor of manhood, a stroke that is most deeply felt by the family, and mourned by a large circle of friends and acquaintances. Trained to habits of industry, active and intelligent, as well as ambitious, he had promised himself much from this world, and few have fairer hopes than he had, of honorable distinction with their fellowmen. But in the midst of fair promises, he was called to contemplate death, to think of the spirit world as near at hand. There is hope that repentance and faith had their perfect work ; that reconciled and renewed, his affections, though late, were set on things above. He has left a devoted wife to mourn thus early, the loss of one on whom she had fixed her dearest earthly hopes and fondest expectations.

FAMILY OF ANSEL E. KINNE.

Ansel E., the eighth son of *Prentice Kinne*, was born May 17th, 1820, received a good common school education, prepared for College at the Cazenovia Seminary at the age of twenty-four, and has spent most of his life in teaching. At the age of twenty-nine. in October, 1849, he married Emma Merrick of Syracuse, N. Y.

From 1855 to 1864 he taught one of the city schools. Receiving an appointment from Gen. Saxton as Superintendent of Freedmen, at Fernandina, Florida, he entered upon its duties in Jan. 1864. In 1865 he removed his family to Florida, remaining there two years in charge of freedmen and their schools when he received the appointment of State Superintendent of Schools for Florida. This appointment was declined and he returned to Syracuse, and in Nov., 1867, re-entered the school room as teacher where he now remains, having taught in Syracuse twenty-two years in all.

There have been born to them seven children, three sons and four daughters; one son and one daughter died in childhood.

Charles W. Kinne, the oldest son, received his education in the schools of Syracuse, ending with the High School. At the age of eighteen he returned to Florida as private secretary to Gov. Reed. At the expiration of Gov. Reed's term of office he returned home and engaged in clerical duties until the spring of 1875, when his health became impaired and for relief was advised to go to Florida. There he somewhat regained his health, and in April, 1877, was married to Elizabeth Reddy, daughter of Rev. Dr. Reddy, of Syracuse, New York. He still resides in Florida, engaged in a large hardware store as bookkeeper. They have one son nearly two years of age, Ansel Reddy Kinne.

Lucius M. Kinne, the second son, born Aug. 1855, also received his education in the schools of Syracuse, ending his school days in the High School. He has been engaged in a bank for eight years and is now teller in the Trust and Deposit Company of Onondaga.

Mary A. Kinne, the eldest daughter, born Sept., 1860; graduated at the High School in June, 1880, and is now finishing her education in doing and learning to do housework.

Kittie E. Kinne, the second daughter, born July, 1862; graduated at the High School in June, 1880, and is now taking a course in a teachers' training class.

Chlobelle Kinne, the third daughter, born June, 1868, is now in her father's school preparing for the High School, which she may enter in 1882, if life and success in preparation are granted her.

These children have responded to the care and culture, such as their parents have been permitted to give them, in a manner that indicates affectionate loyalty to family relation and a proper respect to its claims.

GEORGE N. KINNE.

George N., the ninth son of Prentice Kinne, and by the second marriage, was born Jan. 24th, 1829. Up to the age of ten years he was a smart, active, intelligent boy; at that time his mental as well as his physical powers seemed to pause in their development, and indeed, never resumed a healthy or vigorous growth or improvement.

Soon after his death the following obituary appeared in print, which was truthful to the letter:

DIED.—In Dewitt, Onondaga County, on the 8th of Nov., 1856, of typhoid fever, Mr. George N. Kinne, in the 28th year of his age.

Candor and conscientiousness with entire truthfulness, were elements of character which shone through the life of the deceased. He was religiously inclined from early youth, and in his closing hours evinced a full preparation for the life which is to come. A widowed mother and many relatives and friends are deeply afflicted by this bereavement.

FAMILY OF EZRA KINNE.

Ezra Kinne, eldest son of Cyrus Kinne, was born Jan. 14th, 1778, and came to Manlius, Onondaga County, New York, with his father as stated above. In 1793 he married Mary Young and settled in the same town where they lived and died. Mary, his wife, died in 1824, and Ezra in 1829. Their children, twelve in number, are as follows:

Hannah Kinne, born Feb. 1795, married James Van-Slyke and died in 1823. Two children, Nancy and Emeline.

Aaron Kinne, oldest son of Ezra, was born Oct. 23d, 1796. He married Laura Smith. A jeweller by trade, he followed the business for many years, but in later life, he was a preacher of the Universalist persuasion. He resided in Madison County, New York, for several years and removed to Illinois where he died in 1846. They reared four children, two sons and two daughters.

Harriet, the oldest daughter, was born May 17th, 1820. She married a clergyman in Illinois, Rev. Mr. Gardner.

Melissa, the second daughter, married and lives in Illinois.

Thomas Jefferson, the eldest son of Aaron, was in the war of Secession and held the commissions of captain and colonel, and acquitted himself with honor.

Since the war he has been engaged by the government in various relations to the Revenue Department.

In that connection he now is, and located in Chicago, Illinois.

When mustered out, he was brevetted Brig. Gen. for meritorious conduct.

He was appointed Special Agent of the Revenue Department and visited all the principal cities of the United States.

Elizabeth Kinne, second daughter of Ezra Kinne, was born Jan. 18th, 1799, and married James Breed and died in 1840. They had several children; one is a physician in the west, perhaps two, and are prominent men.

Mary Kinne, third daughter, born Dec. 12th, 1800; married Quartus Frost, had several children, and died in 1835.

Sila Kinne, fourth daughter, born Nov. 16th, 1802. Married Hiram Tisdell Feb., 1834, and died in 1874.

Cyrus Kinne, second son of Ezra, was born Aug. 16th, 1804; married April 25th, 1824, and died Dec. 17th, 1866.

Justus Hull Kinne, third son of Ezra, was born Aug. 3d, 1806; married Prudence Harris Dec., 1831, and died March 26th, 1868. He removed to Illinois early in life and became a substantial, well-to-do farmer. One son, James, was in the war, and was mortally wounded and died in the hospital.

Thomas Jefferson, fourth son of Ezra Kinne, was born May 3d, 1808. He married Ann Sargent; was a jeweler and removed to Illinois about the time his brother did and became the possessor of a fair competence in the pursuit of his trade in Jeilet, Illinois, where in 1872 he died, leaving his widow in the possession and pursuit of his business. She still pursues it and prospers. They had no children. Thomas was social, free-hearted and jolly.

Luke Kinne, fifth son of Ezra, was born June 26th, 1810; married Emeline Stone, a very estimable lady, Dec. 25th, 1831. He was a blacksmith by trade and pursued for many years the trade of his choice. But for forty years he endeavored to preach the Gospel to others. He had been a professor of the faith for many years previous to entering the ministry. He died in the triumph of the faith May 25th, 1880.

He left a widow and several children. His widow still lives and has a home with her youngest son, Sylvester Kinne, at Valparaiso, Indiana.

Sarah Kinne, fifth daughter of Ezra Kinne, was born 1811; married George Hilts, and now lives in Manlius, Onondaga County, New York.

Vasti Kinne, sixth daughter of Ezra Kinne, was born 1814; married Alvin West.

Raphael Kinne, sixth son of Ezra Kinne, was born July 9th, 1817, and married Matilda Kinne, a distant relative. He now lives in Arlington, Knox County, Illinois.

FAMILY OF ZACHARIAH KINNE.

Zachariah Kinne, the second son of Cyrus Kinne, was born Feb. 24th, 1772, in Preston, New London County, Connecticut. At the age of twenty-two years he married Diadama Barnes in Pompey, Onondaga County, New York, May, 1794, and settled in Fayetteville, on or near the farm of his father, in the same month and year. He was temperate, economical, original and somewhat eccentric. He was a farmer, and at his death, which occurred July 1st, 1850, had acquired some property, and assisted to settle his numerous family not remote from his own home. His children were thirteen in number, eight sons and five daughters.

Diana, the eldest daughter, was born May 29th, 1795, and in 1815 married Cromwell Cook and settled in Salina, where she died in 1840, Dec. 25th.

Rite, the oldest son, was born April 1st, 1797, and married Polly Strong Jan. 1st, 1817; settled in DeWitt, Onondaga County, New York, where he died Aug., 1865.

Phineas, the second son, born April 14th, 1799; married Elizabeth Strong, May, 1820; settled in DeWitt; was a miller, and died in Manlius, New York, 1865.

Ira, the third son, died in infancy.

Mary, the second daughter, born 1802; married a Mr.

Cleveland and died 1875, at her daughter's in Syracuse, New York.

Adah, the third daughter, born 1804; married John Keller, settled in Sullivan, Madison County, New York, and died, March, 1873.

Esop, the fourth son, was born July 12th, 1806; married Lydia Beebe; settled on a farm in Salina, now within the city limits of Syracuse, where he died in 1871. He reared a somewhat numerous family of children.

David, is a Baptist minister in Illinois.

La Vega, is a lawyer in Wisconsin.

Gilbert, is a farmer in Michigan.

Lydia, a daughter, married and lives in Syracuse.

Cyrus, born 1808; married Abiah Townsend, settled in DeWitt and now lives in that town.

Rachel, the fourth daughter, married Elisha Eggleston, and died June 18th, 1849, in Canada West.

Barnes, died in infancy.

Lydia, the fifth daughter, born July 15th, 1816; married George Lansing and died Dec. 5th, 1841.

Zachariah, born May 15th, 1818: married Betsey Keller, settled on a farm within the limits of the present city of Syracuse, New York, and now lives in southwestern Michigan.

Benjamin, the youngest son, born May 8th, 1820; married Mary Jane McSchoaler Jan. 29th, 1840, settled in Sullivan, New York, and died in Schroeppel, Oswego County, New York; was a farmer.

FAMILY OF ETHEL KINNE.

Ethel Kinne, the fourth son of Cyrus Kinne, was born April 3d, 1775, and died Jan. 30th, 1857, at the age of 82 years. He married Betsey Eaton; he settled in Manlius, Onondaga County, but removed to Cicero, where he lived and died.

Parsons, his oldest son, was born September 17th, 1797, and married Phœbe Landers, who was born Dec. 13th, 1798, and has a numerous family.

Lewis lives in Palermo, Oswego County, New York.

Levi, second son, lives in Brewerton, Onondaga County, New York.

Betsey Ann lives in Clyde.

Juliet lives in Brewerton.

Ethel is a farmer and lives in DeWitt, Onondaga County.

Harvey lives in Michigan.

Abula, unmarried, lives with her brother Ethel.

Hannah lives in Brewerton.

Salome lives at Blodgett's Mills, Cortland County.

Palmer Kinne, second son of Ethel Kinne, married a Miss Porter; had six children, viz: Sophronia, Chester, Eliza, Riley, Charles P. and Esther.

Sophronia married Mr. Lasher, and lives in Chicago.

Chester went west; is a lawyer in Chicago.

Riley died sometime ago.

Charles P. lives in Illinois.

Eliza lives in Chicago, as also *Esther*.

Abulah, only daughter of Ethel Kinne, married Jonathan Emmons and resides in Chicago, Illinois.

Jackson, third son of Ethel Kinne, married Mary Jane Veder; had two children. Married again and had one child. Children all dead. Father and children died in the west.

Harry, youngest son of Ethel Kinne, married Susan Waite; had six children; lives in Camden, Oneida County, New York.

FAMILY OF ZEBULON KINNE.

Zebulon Kinne, fifth son of Cyrus Kinne and twin brother of Moses Kinne, was born Jan. 12th, 1780, in Rensselaer County, New York. Came to Onondaga at the age of twelve years with his father. He married Lucy Markham and settled on a farm in Manlius, now DeWitt, Onondaga County. During his majority and previous to his marriage, he commenced clearing a farm near the present village of Brewerton, but soon purchased the farm of 180 acres, situate as above, and on which the village of East Syracuse now stands. They reared eight children, four sons and four daughters.

Manassah, the oldest son, died in his minority.

James, the second son, married Miss Hay and settled on a farm near Belle Isle, Onondaga County. He left the farm about 1860; it is not known, if living, where he is. No children were born to them.

Rufus R., third son of Zebulon, born about 1820 or '21; married Miss Julia Clark, of Salina; settled with his father, at whose death, which occurred Aug., 1865, Rufus came in possession, by will, of the homestead and farm, under conditions and provisions respecting the other members of the family. By the locating of East Syracuse the farm became very valuable, much of it is now occupied by dwellings, stores, railroad shops, &c.

He was a stirring business man; was a Democrat in polities, and a kind husband and father. He died in the spring of 1880, leaving a widow and one daughter. A little son died in infancy some years ago.

Chester, fourth son of Zebulon Kinne, was married, and one of the children, a young man of twenty, now lives in Montana, a bright, active and promising young man. His father, Chester Kinne, resides with one of the sisters in the western part of this State.

Lucy, the oldest daughter, married Mr. Pendleton, and after his death a Mr. Dallaby. She has no children. She is a very energetic, business woman; now resides in Brockport, New York.

Emeline, the second daughter of Zebulon, married Mr. Palmer; they now reside in the western part of the State of New York.

Elizabeth, the third daughter, married a physician, by whom she had some children. She became impaired in health of body and mind and is now residing and has lived for years, a helpless dependant at the old homestead, cared for during their lives by her father and mother, and provided for in the will of her father.

Olivia, the fourth daughter, married Mr. Kent; has lived in Syracuse, New York, many years, and is now residing in Rochester with her second husband, a Mr. Hammond.

Zebulon Kinne died at the age of eighty-five years. Mrs. Kinne survived him only a few days. Mr. Kinne, for several years previous to his marriage, lived with and labored for his brother Prentice, on the farm. And, as their farms adjoined, an unusual and fraternal intimacy existed and continued many years. The families of these brothers, Prentice and Zebulon, long after the death of Prentice, continued to live near each other and in very intimate and friendly relation. Mr. Kinne was a man of strong purposes and will, generally just—always kind. For many years previous to his death he was a member of the First Baptist Church of Syracuse. He was so proverbially kind to every body that many, irrespective of the relation which the word conveys, called him " Uncle."

FAMILY OF MOSES KINNE.

Moses Kinne, the seventh son of Cyrus Kinne, was born June 12th, 1780, in Rensselaer County, New York; removed with his father to Fayetteville, Onondaga County, New York, March 14th, 1803. He married Betsey Williams and settled in Cicero, Onondaga County, and died in Euclid in the town of Clay, formerly Cicero, New York, September 20th, 1855, being seventy-five years of age. There were born to them ten children, four sons and six daughters.

Abigail, the oldest daughter, born Jan. 17th, 1804; married Ephraim Soule and settled in Euclid, New York, and died March 4th, 1856, in the town of Salina, New York. Her husband, Mr. Soule, was the maker of the "Sovereign Balm Pill," so well and widely known throughout this and other States for its excellent remedial properties. He was a man of wealth and influence.

Moses Kinne, jr., the second child and oldest son of Moses Kinne, sen., was born Aug. 15th, 1805, and married Polly Warner; was a farmer; settled in Clay, where he died, July 5th, 1852.

Albern, the second son, born Oct. 17th, 1807; married Phœbe Breed Oct. 10th, 1832; settled in Clay, where they had two children born to them, a son and a daughter. Allen B. and Julia. He died at Woodard, Onondaga County, New York, where his children still reside, May 12th, 1879.

Amanda, the second daughter, born Nov. 4th, 1809; married William Hale and settled in Belgium, New York.

Harriet, third daughter, born Nov. 21st, 1811; married Samuel Lounsbury and settled in Belgium, New York.

Almira, fourth daughter of Moses Kinne, Esq., born Oct. 17th, 1813; married a Mr. Way, in Euclid, 1833, and died in Detroit, Michigan, 1868.

Jerome, third son, born Aug. 2d, 1818, married Harriet Soule; and settled in Schroeppel, Oswego County, New York. He was a farmer.

Ora, fifth daughter, born Jan., 1819; married Daniel Warner; settled in Palermo, New York, where she died, 1841.

Julia, sixth daughter, born Jan. 21st, 1821; married a Mr. Kore in 1845; settled in 1855 in Hadley, Michigan.

Frank, youngest son, born May 22d, 1822; married Mrs. Euretta Foster in 1849, and settled in Syracuse, but removed to Hudson, Michigan, where he died in 1872.

Moses Kinne was a member of the Legislature in, 1825, associate of the late James R. Lawrence. He held the offices of Supervisor and Justice of the Peace in his town. Upright in character, dignified in bearing, he was held in respect by the community in which he lived and died. (See app.)

FAMILY OF JOSHUA KINNE.

Joshua Kinne was born in Steventown, Rensselaer County, New York, Aug. 31st, 1782. At the age of twenty-three he was united in marriage with Miss Melinda Leach, of Pompey, Onondaga County, and soon after removed to Cicero, in the same county, where he commenced preaching and where he probably professed religion. In 1815 he removed to Marion, Wayne County, where he was ordained, and served the church there as pastor twelve years. About 1830 he moved to Greece, Monroe County, and served the church at that place seven years. Here, in 1832, his wife died, and in 1833 he married Mrs. Diantha Bennett. Removing from Greece, he resided in Sodus some years, preaching in Ontario and Williamson.

About 1843 he removed to Fairfield, Lenawee County, Michigan. For fifteen years he preached in the several places, Lodi, Nankin, Unadilla, Waterloo and LeRoy. He died at LeRoy, Oct. 17th, 1858, in the seventy-seventh year of his age. He rode on horseback eight miles, preached, and returned, the Sunday before his death. There were born to him four sons and four daughters. *Moses P.*, the oldest son, was born Jan. 10th, 1805; *Susannah*, the oldest daughter, was born March 3d, 1806; *Rachel*, born Jan. 24th, 1808; *Niles*, born Sept. 26th, 1809; *Sily*, born Feb. 3d, 1811; *Melinda*, born Aug. 30th, 1812; *Afred B.*, born Dec. 26th, 1815; *Joshua, jr.*, born May 19th, 1817.

Moses P., the oldest son, married and settled in Medina, Michigan. He was a farmer, and died a few years since over seventy years of age, leaving two daughters.

Susannah, the oldest daughter, married Reuben Simmons, and settled in the vicinity of Ottawa, Illinois. They now reside at Guthrie Center, Iowa. They have a large family.

Rachel married Welcome Porter, and settled in a place on the border of Oneida Lake, where she died in 1830, leaving two children; one of these, Cyrus Kinne Porter, resides in Buffalo, New York, is an architect of the firm of Porter & Percival.

Niles, born in Cicero, Onondaga County, New York; born again while a little child, probably not more than six years old, but did not profess religion until about 1831. He first united with the Baptist Church in Greece, Monroe County, being baptized by his father. About fourteen years of his early manhood were occupied in teaching. He was licensed to preach by the First Baptist Church, of Rochester, New York, and was there ordained Aug. 28th, 1844. In Sept. he removed with his family to Milwaukee, Wisconsin, and in Feb., 1845, entered upon his first pastorate at Beloit. Here he remained until July, 1850, and had the joy of seeing a church of twenty-five members increased to more than two hundred, and left them with the best church edifice in the town. His next pastorate was at St. Charles, Kane County, Illinois. His labors as a minister from that time to the present have been in Illinois, with the exception of one year at Grass Lake, Michigan.

He has served the following churches as pastor, viz; Barry, Pittsfield twice, Carrolton, Oak Mill, Lebanon, Troy, Payson, Carthage twice, Bushnell, and now New Canton. His education was obtained in the public schools, Palmyra, New York, High School, and at Rochester Collegiate Institute. In 1833 he was married to Miss Ruth H. Rowe, who died Aug., 1835, leaving a son, now living in Beloit, Wisconsin. He is a baker by trade. In 1837 he was married a second time, to Miss Williams, of Greece, Monroe County, New York. Six children were born to them, three sons and three daughters. Three died in infancy. *Abijah Theodore*, the oldest son living, is a deacon in the Baptist Church, resides in Barry, and is now employed in the Exchange Bank in that town. *Niles Henry*, the second son, spent three years in the army during the war for the Union; is now a farmer living four miles south of Barry. The only daughter living is Mrs. Scarborough. All three of the children are members of the Baptist Church, both the sons being deacons.

Melinda, the youngest daughter of Joshua Kinne, married Ezra D. Lay, and now lives at Ypsilanti, Michigan. Mr. Lay is a wealthy farmer, an elder in the Presbyterian Church, and has been a member of the Legislature of Michigan. His wife and daughter are still members of the Baptist Church. They have only a son and daughter living.

Alfred B., born in Cicero, Onondaga County, New York, was two years old when his father removed to Marion, Wayne County, New York. In 1830 he made a profession of religion and united with the Baptist Church in the town of Greece, Monroe County, New York. In 1836 he married Miss Harriet M. Bennett in Palmyra, New York. In 1842 was licensed to preach by the Baptist Church, of Sodus, New York. In 1845 he moved to Michigan, and in 1848 was ordained, and was pastor of the following churches, viz: Marion, Livingston Co., Dansville, Ingham Co., Leroy and Williamston, of the same county, Belleville, Wayne Co. Mrs. Kinne died in Williamston, March 26th, 1872. There were born to them four sons and two daughters. The daughters died young. A son, *Cyrus Adelbert*, was killed at Brentwood, Tennessee, May 21st, 1863, aged 21 years, while a Union soldier in the service of his country. *Newton Irving, Elliott Bennett* and *Lewis Judson*, sons of Alfred B. Kinne, are still living. Newton I. and Elliott B. are married, and reside in Lake County, Michigan; the former having one son and three daughters, the latter one son. Lewis Judson still lives with his father, who was married the second time in July, 1880, to Lucy Stanly, and now resides in the city of Lansing, Michigan.

Joshua, jr., the youngest son of the Rev. Joshua Kinne, was born in Marion, Wayne Co., New York, 1817; was married in Plymouth, Wayne Co., Michigan, to Miss Mary A. Blanchard, April, 1841, by whom he had two sons, *Alonzo* and *Melvin*, both of whom are still living. Alonzo is married and resides in Williamston, Michigan, and has three sons. Mr. Joshua Kinne, jr., died in the hospital at Stephenson, Alabama, Dec. 27th, 1864, forty-seven years of age, while serving in the Union army.

FAMILY OF CYRUS KINNE, JR.

Cyrus Kinne, Jr. the eighth son of Cyrus, sen., was given a farm of a hundred acres, but never settled upon it. His father had begun the erection of a saw-mill before his death, which occurred in the year 1808. Cyrus chose to remain at the old homestead, in the care of his mother. He completed the erection of the saw-mill and busied himself on the farm and at the mill for several years, and during this time married Asenath Warner, and commenced housekeeping near where his mill was located. There were born to them five children. He died in the summer of 1824, while, in point of years, in the prime of life. He was an active man and in intellect equal to either of his brothers. He was the first one of the ten sons stricken in death.

Samantha, his oldest daughter, married Felix Fralick in Oswego Co., N. Y. They had five children; two daughters only, Armantha and Letitia, lived to become adults. The older married Mr. Ostrander, in Oswego Co., and the younger a Mr. Benedict of the same county, and now lives in Eaton Co., Mich.

Diantha L. Kinne married N. Hildreth Kinne, son of Prentice Kinne, whose record has been given in preceding pages.

Fidelia, the youngest daughter, married a Mr. Perry and removed to Sunfield, Mich., many years ago and died soon after her arrival leaving no children.

K. Hiram Kinne, son of Cyrus Kinne, jr., married Sarah Cheever, and four children were born to them, viz: Eldora, died in infancy; Cyrus, 3d, died young; Alice, now Mrs. Mills, lives in Muskegon, Mich., and another Eldora lives with her aunt, Diantha L., her parents, Hiram and Sarah, having died many years ago.

FAMILY OF JAPHETH KINNE.

Japheth Kinne, the ninth son of Cyrus Kinne, at the age of nine years removed to Manlius with his father. At the age of twenty-one he returned to Rensselaer County and labored on a farm by the month. In April, 1807, he married Temperance Palmer by whom he had nine children, only four of whom—two sons and two daughters, reached manhood and womanhood. In 1808 he returned to Onondaga County and in 1810 settled on a hundred acres of land in the town of Cicero, given him by his father Cyrus. Here he lived for more than twenty-five years. In 1836 or '37 he removed to Ira, Cayuga County, N. Y., where he bought a farm and where he lived eight years, and then removed to Oswego County, N. Y. Here, in 1857, his wife died. In 1858, at the age of seventy-five, he married the widow Huyke, an acquaintance and friend of his youth, with whom he lived seven years, when she died. His sons, Darius and Uri, had removed to Michigan and died. His youngest daughter had married Mr. Walsh and also removed to Michigan. His daughter Roxana, married Mr. Benedict and still lived in Oswego County. In 1865 Japheth Kinne sold his farm and removed to Michigan with his daughters; his sons having died he resided with the daughters alternately until 1868, when Mrs. Walsh died. The father continued to reside with his daughter, Mrs. Benedict, until 1873, when at the age of eighty-seven years he also died. The daughter still lives (in 1881) where the father died, at Bismarck, Michigan.

In all the years of early pioneer life, amid the hardships incident thereto, in changes, in afflictions, in middle manhood and in age, Japheth Kinne bore himself steadily in the strong fortitude of a Christian faith. About 1825 he united with the Baptist Church of Cicero, and was chosen deacon and as such served many years. In the division of the town the church was also divided and a new church organized in the new town of Clay. Mr. Kinne was elected deacon and clerk of the new church and was continued so long as he lived in the town. He held several offices of trust, but never sought political notoriety.

FAMILY OF PALMER KINNE.

Palmer Kinne, the tenth and youngest son of Cyrus Kinne, was not of age when his father died, but was provided for by will, with one hundred acres of land lying in the township of Cicero. He married Polly Carr, settled on his land and for several years resided thereon, and in 1835 removed to Illinois. There were eleven children born to them, some of whom died in childhood.

Cynthia L. Kinne, the oldest child, born Feb. 11th, 1811; married LeRoy Hudson in 1840.

De Witt D. Kinne, died in childhood.

Caleb P. Kinne, born May 10th, 1814; was in the Union army in the South three years, and died in 1873.

Eli M. Kinne, born April 12th, 1816; married Maria Heath in 1839, by whom he had Warner C. Kinne. In 1847 he was again married to Laura Fisk and had by her Palmer F. Kinne.

Mary Ann Kinne, born April 12th, 1818; died Sept. 13th, 1840.

David L. Kinne died in childhood.

Warner N. Kinne also died young.

Sylvanus H. Kinne, born Feb. 7th, 1824; married Mary Austin by whom he had twelve children.

Susan J. Kinne, born March 16th, 1826; married Norman C. Fisk in 1851, by whom she had Norman L. Fisk in 1852. In the same year Mr. Fisk, her husband, died. In 1858 Mrs. Fisk married Orrin Stafford by whom she had four children. The eldest, Maria, (Minnie) A. Stafford, now a young lady of twenty-two years, very kindly furnished much and indeed most of the material of this, her grandfather's record. The writer well remembers little Minnie when visiting at her father's house fifteen years since.

Eliza H. Kinne, the fourth daughter and tenth child, was born June 3d, 1828.

Maria C. Kinne, the fifth daughter and youngest child of Palmer Kinne, born March 24th, 1832; married Ethan Carpenter Oct., 1857, by whom she had four children.

Pliny P. Hudson, son of Cynthia L. Hudson and grandson of Palmer Kinne, was in the war of the Rebellion nearly a year.

Sylvanus H. Kinne was in the Mexican war a short time.

Eli M. Kinne was Postmaster and Justice of the Peace, and was in company with his brother-in-law, Mr. Carpenter, many years since.

Illinois is the State in which most of Palmer Kinne's numerous descendants reside. He died Nov. 15th, 1869, his wife having died July 18th, 1865.

FAMILY OF RACHEL KINNE.

Rachel Kinne, the oldest daughter of Zachariah Kinne, married William Williams; settled on land a little east of Manlius Center. Here she died leaving four children, two sons and two daughters. Mr. Williams married again but died soon after.

The elder son, *Kinne Williams*, married and settled in the town of Cicero. Several children were born to them. His sons have attained to honorable distinction and positions in society.

The second son, *Ezra Williams*, as a boy and as a man was very industrious. He married and settled in the old township of Manlius; here his wife died. Since then he has been twice married and has resided in various localities, and is now a resident of one of the western States.

The oldest daughter of Rachel Kinne, named *Anna*, married Mr. Haywood who settled on a farm near Kirkville. A son now occupies the farm—both parents deceased.

The second daughter of Rachel (Kinne) Williams, *Comfort*, married Collins Bunnell. They reared a family of children. The mother died and Mr. Bunnell married again and moved, some years ago, to the State of Illinois.

FAMILY OF COMFORT KINNE.

Comfort Kinne, the youngest daughter of Cyrus Kinne, was married to Jacob Springsted. They were provided with a farm in the town of Cicero, Onondaga Co., N. Y. There were born to them several children. Mr. Springsted was a very industrious man, a good husband and a kind father. About the year 1820 he moved into the western part of this State, and soon after into the State of Illinois where all knowledge of them to the writer is lost.

I regret that a fuller record, which Mr. Springsted well deserves, is beyond my reach.

REMINISCENCES OF MOSES KINNE.

Moses Kinne, together with his twin brother, Zebulon, opened his eyes upon the light in Stonington, Connecticut, Monday, June 12th, 1780, little more than 101 years ago. It was said that of the two babies Moses was much the smaller, though in mature life seemed as robust and was certainly superior in weight and size. Very few incidents of his early life can be recalled at this late date. An occurrence, which doubtless had much influence on his life, took place in his fifteenth year. He was in the fallow where the men were busy logging when, a log being in readiness to place on the pile, an older brother requested him to lift one end. The sudden and violent exertion caused the breaking of a blood vessel. A severe hemorrhage followed that reduced his strength alarmingly. When able to endure the fatigue of travel, a sojourn at the seaside with ocean baths twice a day, was advised. He spent a year there, returning greatly improved in health; his system, however, not recovering its normal tone for some years.

The will of Cyrus Kinne, a copy of which is before me, mentions Moses as his sixth son; six other children came into this already large family, and one can readily imagine there were many steps to be taken by somebody, consequently Moses, on account of being less able than his brothers to perform outdoor labor, was often called upon to aid his mother in her household duties, frequently doing the family washing. Tradition hath it that upon one occasion the ruffled cotton shirt—a choice possession in those days of homespun—belonging to his oldest brother, Zachariah, was put in the kettle with the linen sheets, shirts, pantaloons, etc., and all "boiled up" together in lye, the favorite "cleansing fluid" of those early times, and one, that while "whitening" linen, tended to "yellow" cotton, it at least rendered this particular shirt so dingy that Zachariah looked upon it as ruined, and proceeded to chastise Moses after the approved method then in vogue. But whether he ever discovered to what he owed the disaster that had occurred to his treasure, whether to accident or sly humor on the part of the washer-boy, narrator failed to state. It might have been that the garment, being an important factor in the owner's "sparking" outfit, offered itself as a temptation to "tease" not easily resisted.

From the fact that Moses was employed so much in household tasks may have arisen his interest in women's work, so called, for in his own home he gave a helping hand on many occasions that to most men do not present themselves. The labor of frying cakes he always took upon himself when not otherwise occupied, his daughters mixing and rolling out, for owing to appliances connected with a fire-place and used in the work, it was, he considered, too laborious for the women. Yet he was heard to say in his later life that he did not then realize how much he could assist already heavily burdened hands, in ways that cost him very little effort. This kindness and thoughtfulness for women did not at all impair his dignity, nor did he seem to fear that it would, should it come to the knowledge of other men.

It was said that he once thought seriously of studying medicine for which he had a predilection. What changed his mind was not related. He was married in early life, 1802, at twenty-two, to Elizabeth or Betsey Williams, born at Windham, Connecticut, May 30th, 1782, and who came into Manlius from Vermont, her adopted State, with a married sister. As it was then no disgrace to work out, she found employment in Cyrus Kinne's family, where Moses became acquainted with her. It would be interesting to know how much she received a week; wages were not high—teachers of the best grades getting only ten or twelve shillings a week, house help, perhaps half that. She has been described as the "smartest" girl in her neighborhood, working always rapidly and with judgment. The young couple, after marriage, remained with the old people a few months, then began housekeeping in Locke, Cayuga County, where their two oldest children, Abigail and Moses, were born. They lived in Locke only three years, removing thence upon 150 acres in Cicero, afterwards Clay, Onondaga County. The place now called Euclid occupies the south part of said farm, then a wilderness. The clearing made at that time being the first in the central part of the town, others following immediately.

As an incident of those early times, and remembered in connection with the events of that year, it was stated that soon after the removal of the family to their future home in early autumn of 1806, a deep snow fell, Oct. 17th, and receiving additions from time to time did not finally disappear till the following February. Not a very inviting prospect, certainly, but there was much to be done and the first winter was consumed in settling, in adjusting themselves to the new order of things and becoming acquainted with neighbors and surroundings. Yet they were not among strangers entirely for a family named Lynn accompanied them from Manlius, purchasing within a mile or two of them. Within the next three years two brothers, Palmer and Japheth, and a sister, Comfort, located in the same town. At first the family dwelt in a log house of a very comfortable and roomy style, which, after eight or ten years, proving too small for the wants of the increasing numbers, gave way for a spacious frame dwelling, that after more than sixty-five years is doing good service as a section of a very modern house.

The second and third winters he (Moses) taught school, also in a log house; in summer found plenty of occupation in clearing off and logging—piling up logs preparatory to burning, at which he was called a good hand, for even in the apparently simple matter of piling logs good judgment comes in play. But particularly was he famous at breaking and driving oxen, seldom or never meeting with an accident—practice in guiding them among the stumps doubtless giving him aptness. Indeed, in all feats of strength and skill, dear to the heart of the frontiersman, he took the lead. The prestige thus gained may have smoothed the road for him to political preferment, as he began his public career soon after his settlement in his new home; serving first as Justice, then as Supervisor, which office he filled acceptably eighteen years, and during that time served one term in the Legislature.

It is stated that one of his first official acts as Justice was marrying a couple on the opposite side of the Oneida river in Oswego County, a mile distant. In the evening, discussing the event with his brother-in-law, Joseph Williams, a shrewd politician, it was concluded that the ceremony was illegal, because out of his jurisdiction, and the two proceeded immediately to the river that divides the two counties where Mr. W. procured a boat and rowing across—the only method at that time and for some years after—he aroused the pair, it being 10 o'clock P. M., to whom he briefly explained, and returned with them to the waiting justice, who then and there legalized his work. As each of the party was desirous of keeping the matter secret it was a surprise to hear it publicly mentioned, and wonder being expressed as to how it came out, it was found there had been a listener concealed in the grass.

When entering upon his political life he affiliated with the Loco Focos, but afterward saw fit to join the ranks of the Whigs. It was at this time he was elected to the Legislature as a party expression of satisfaction at his course, no doubt, in turning to them in his strength.

As he occupied the position of supervisor so long he had an extensive acquaintance and was well known through a wide extent of territory. People in that day of few neighbors were not deterred from social intercourse by distance or lack of facilities that seem to us great.

When he began on his farm in Cicero the site of Syracuse was an impenetrable cedar swamp, and no one predicted, not even the boldest, it would be the most valuable section in Central New York, consequently it was avoided by those selecting land. Yet he once thought of buying at, or near there before purchasing in Cicero.

Not a long time has elapsed since many were living who were the associates of Moses Kinne in his public life. Among them Gen. J. R. Lawrence, who conversed several times with his son, Albern, and recalled with much interest incidents of their work when both were in the Legislature together, and of their journeys to and from the capital, when journeying was not quite so easily accomplished as now. He also spoke of him as an able man and much respected by his party. Concerning his domestic life, it is remembered that while exacting obedience he was ever a tender father, and though compelled from pressure of public duties to be absent much, his home was ever in his mind. This home was not that originally carved out of the wilderness. That had long before been sold and another house built near the "corners," as Euclid was familiarly known.

To this home were many visitors, strangers and friends, welcomed.

His wife, in her later years, was an invalid, and her room next to the family room and nearly as large, was really the social center for the married sons and daughters who came often to spend an hour or day with "mother," or to consult with the father. Nearly all lived within an hour's drive and some in the same place. Of the ten sons and daughters only two were unmarried at the time of their mother's death, which took place in 1844. She left a memory fragrant of good deeds and devoted piety.

After the death of his wife his youngest daughter married, and he soon after sold the homestead to his son-in-law, E. L. Soule, taking up his abode with his widowed daughter, Mrs. Lounsbury, thereafter dividing his time and what little labor he felt himself able to perform between his children, ever retaining until the last, a warm interest in each household, even to its least and youngest member. I have, myself, seen him put himself to much inconvenience to wait upon his married daughters, not at all because they were in need, but because it gave him pleasure. About four years previous to his death three daughters, Mrs. Hale, Way and Kone, moved to Michigan, and he twice made the journey to assure himself of their welfare, the last time driving the entire distance. While there he contracted chill fever, and returning home lived only a week, dying at the advanced age of seventy-five years.

It is not known whether Mr. Kinne ever became a member of any church, but his sympathies were with the Christian or Disciple church of which his wife was a member. His religious experience dates from the time of Elder Moriell's work in Euclid when a church of that denomination was organized there. Ministers of other persuasions sought his friendly home, and he extended aid to all religious enterprises in the community.

A Baptist Church was built on a lot of his, given for the purpose, and whenever a meeting of more than usual importance was held in it those from a distance were sure of entertainment at 'Squire Kinne's house. His impressive manner and fitting words in devotion are well remembered, his forgiving spirit gratefully borne in mind. It is a source of gratification to those of his children and grandchildren who remain, to reflect that this long and useful career, while destitute of startling events, was one of unblemished reputation politically, that his private life was unstained by any irregularity, that though trials of various kinds assailed him, and death twice entered his household, he was still cheerful, companionable and seemed always relying on strength Divine.

My recollection of his personal appearance is of a tall, erect, stately frame fully six feet in height, broad-shouldered, rather deep-chested, surmounted by a shapely head, face deeply furrowed yet not rendered repulsive thereby, keen blue or gray-blue eyes, overhanging brows, smoothly shaven and dimpled chin, hair quite gray, very thin and approaching baldness on the top of the head; his bearing was dignified almost to austerity. In conversation instructive and entertaining, unsullied by any coarse allusions of whatever nature, possessing a fund of anecdote and wit and well informed on current topics, though not given to mere book lore. In dress and habits quiet, neat and orderly and always the gentleman. Some speak of him as having been fine looking—I think he was.

His daughter, Mrs. Hale, adds that her father "carried the domestic habits of his early training through life, and always, when upon arising and building the fire, put everything in readiness for getting the breakfast, (his older sons, Moses and Albern, performed these offices while they remained at home.) He was ever a kind and devoted husband, and during her mother's long illness was tender, and watchful as any mother of her child, and never, when entering the house from business or labor, paused till within the sick room and had taken a seat near her. A kind and indulgent parent always anxious for the welfare and happiness of his family, and a genial neighbor and friend to all in need."

It is not claimed that the subject of this sketch was without a fault, but the same grave covers both them and his mortal frame. J. K.

APPENDIX.

C. MASON KINNE.

The Grand Army of the Republic, based on the best ideas of this nation, viz: the tender memories of the patriot dead, a bond of union of honorably discharged soldiers of the Union, and on the high purpose to preserve and perpetuate the honor and glory of our country soundly saved from domestic discord, civil anarchy and ruin at the hands of its disloyal citizens, is broad enough to unite and enroll in its membership more than a hundred thousand of the patriotic defenders of the country.

Gen. Grant, President Garfield and a host of commanding generals are members of the organization. The whole country is reached by its influence. Its Departments and its Posts cover the largest and best area of the country. In the California Department alone there are seventeen Posts. The Commander of this Department is Col. C. Mason Kinne, elected to the position in 1880 and re-elected in 1881. He was a member of the first Post established on the California coast. His early history has been briefly given in the body of this work. His courage and patriotism are preserved in the country's records and the hearts of his comrades in arms. But in the citizen walks of life his talent and his tact find ample field for development and useful exercise. Active and energetic in the pursuit of a responsible and lucrative calling, he still finds time to gratify an unconquerable thirst for investigation of scientific subjects. He is now the President of the San Francisco Microscopical Society, and as a member of that society his investigations in the past years have, through the society, found easy access to the columns of the papers and ready acceptance with men of even riper years and experience, and show a very careful and accurate observation of the minute and the beautiful of creation. He loves to lift the veil and peer into the hidden treasures that refuse revelation to all but the eager and appreciative. He has exploded the long accepted theory that the fly walks the ceiling by atmospheric pressure, and some of the school books that contained this theory have had it expunged therefrom.

He is the designer of a beautiful and imposing monument erected in the Soldiers' Cemetery of San Francisco at a cost of $20,000. It stands on a base on which is inscribed,
  " To the Memory of California's Patriotic Dead, Who
        Served During the War for the Union.
              ' Mustered Out.' "

The monument itself, is a cannon in a vertical position, mouth upward, holding a cannon ball bearing an eagle with spread pinions and looking skyward. Beside the monument stands the goddess, Patriotism, with one arm resting on its pedestal and one foot on its basal ledge, her whole figure embowered with floral wreaths.

At the erection of this monument in 1872, very interesting ceremonies were witnessed. Among the speakers on that occasion was Col. C. M. Kinne. His address was so full of history of the war from 1863 to the surrender in 1865, so graphically drawn, so replete with patriotic sentiments that it deserves a permanent place, but its length and the purposes of this record forbid its insertion herein. Its closing paragraphs must suffice:

" We can show our appreciation of the devotion of those who freely gave their lives for the land they loved, by a hatred of disloyalty and its adherents everywhere. It is well to forgive the traitor his sins; give him the rights of citizenship; let general amnesty be his; permit him to aspire to the highest positions of honor and trust, but there—— stop. Remember that 'eternal vigilance is the price of liberty,' and that having been weighed in the balance and found wanting, we must allow more than a decade to elapse before we give him the power to betray us again.

" It may do for some to prate of our brave but misguided Southern brethren, and claim the courage with which they fought as adding to the valor of a great nation; but there the meagre sentiment ends, and when they ask us to forget traitorous deeds and shake hands over the graves of our loyal martyrs, they ask too much.

" Sentiment may do for to-day, but to-morrow—and tomorrow, and until this Memorial Day comes again and again, we are 'on guard' with fixed bayonets, and without the staunch old countersign 'Loyalty,' none shall pass.

" There are those who would 'sink the soldier and forget the very word,' but from the heart of a just and grateful people swells the mighty surge of recollection, bearing on its crest the memory of the days when defeat followed defeat until our very existence as a nation was jeopardized, and sympathizers with the Rebellion sent word to our boys to come home, allow the Union to be broken and 'let our wayward sisters go in peace.' They may remember that the loyal sons of the North sent back quite another answer —sent up another shout: 'We are coming, we are coming, three hundred thousand more!' giving our army a new and mighty impulse. Thinking bayonets decreed that the nation was not to die, and swelled the thinned ranks of our battered armies. Then Sheridan rode down from Winchester and sent the braggart Early whirling up the valley. Thomas hurled Hood and his legions from the heights about Nashville. Sherman hewed a pathway forty miles wide, from Atlanta to the sea; and Grant, the master mind, controlling all, though ten thousand shells burst beneath his feet, and a tempest of bullets whistled around his head, never loosed his grasp on Lee's throat till the final surrender under the old apple tree at Appomattox.

"There are those who would take into full fellowship the traitor; but memory brings up before us a peaceful, prosperous people plunged into a fratricidal war, that a slave oligarchy might dictate to the world from the throne of King Cotton. But we realize the fact, that the public faith and credit will not be maintained by trusting, *now*, those who did all they could, *then*, to destroy it, and who covertly advocated repudiation, or the assumption of their own hell-begotten debts. That the services of the Union soldiers and sailors will not be remembered or honorably requited if we school ourselves to regard the Rebel as their peer. That the rights of four millions of citizens will not be guaranteed if their traitor masters, who fought to bind firmer their bonds, are regarded as worthy of *utter forgiveness* and national confidence."

In youth and manhood, in war and in peace, C. M. Kinne has sustained a worthy record.

WESLEY BAILEY.

Wesley Bailey, by marriage with the eldest daughter of Prentice Kinne, became identified with the Kinne family in 1833. The family record, now under the eye of the writer, relates: that on the 14th day of August, in that year, Wesley Bailey, son of Elder Elijah Bailey, was united to Eunice Kinne, daughter of Prentice Kinne, by Elder Allen, of the Baptist Church in Syracuse, and that the event occurred in Manlius, since DeWitt, in the county of Onondaga.

Wesley Bailey, born in Readsville, Vermont, in 1808, had come to DeWitt, the home of the Kinnes, in the years previous, as a teacher of the district school. To the school, with her taller and well grown brothers, came Eunice, their eldest sister, and after their mother's death, their chief dependence in the home circle. The new teacher was light-hearted and companionable, and easily established good relations with those under his charge. For some of them it was afterwards much easier to understand how he had gained their regard, than to understand how he had won the affection of their elder and sedate sister. He was sanguine; she was sober, earnest—not too prone to look on the brightest side. How much of the earnestness, sincerity and conscientiousness afterwards exhibited as a part of his character, was due to the companionship which began in the year of their marriage, cannot be computed; but that the union was a happy, and in all respects a fortunate one, cannot be doubted. Such qualifications as he needed for the ministry, in which his father was a figure of some note, he completed soon after his marriage.

In 1838 he was a Reformed Methodist preacher in South Cortland, Cortland Co., and the editor of a religious journal with the old-fashioned title of *The South Cortland Luminary.* When, two years later, he went to Fayetteville, Onondaga Co., he removed his publication office and conducted his paper there during his residence in that village, and his ministry at the neighboring point known as the High Bridge.

The editor, from conviction and study, became an Abolitionist before he came to Fayetteville, and he gave no little attention in his columns to the discussion of the iniquity of human slavery. He was at his desk when a messenger came from the then young city of Utica, representing that great man, Alvan Stewart, requesting Mr. Bailey's removal to Utica, and his assumption of the duty of conducting the Abolition journal, which had recently been mobbed for its earnest utterances. The eminent Abolitionist had read but two of the issues of the Fayetteville journal, but had been impressed with the pointed, happy and effective way in which Mr. Bailey put forth his views on the subject near to Mr. Stewart's heart. There was the earnestness of Garrison, but a tact of which he was incapable. There was the sincerity of Goodell and Beriah Green, but it came to the eye and sense of the leader with an attractive side.

"That is the man we want," said the able Abolitionist, lawyer and orator. " Go and bring him to Utica." The messenger was successful, and in the fall of 1842 Mr. Bailey, with much encouragement, but with no assistance beyond the good will of his Abolition friends, began the publication of an anti-slavery journal in Utica,—*The Liberty Press*, successor to *The Friend of Man.* Not to be mobbed;

not to make enemies. For it belonged neither to his experience nor to his nature to make enemies by his always good-humored, but effective way, of offering his opinions to the public.

Until the close of 1848, he continued his labors as an Abolitionist, and then, foreseeing in the awakened conscience of the country, the doom of slavery, and led to take note of the evils of intemperance, he changed the name of his paper from *The Liberty Press* to *The Utica Teetotaller*. He continued these journals until he was elected State's Prison Inspector by the Republican party in 1856, when he resigned its management to his second son, in order that he might conscientiously give his whole time to the State which, by a commanding vote, had asked his services. For three years, inspired with the best wish to help the unfortunate and the erring, he served the State of New York, and at the close of his service he removed to Iowa with his wife and two younger sons; starting a paper in the enterprising city of Decorah, only to relinquish its labors as these two sons came to his relief and assumed the duties his cheerful spirit was none too ready to relinquish.

Eunice Kinne Bailey, his faithful and devoted wife, died in Decorah in April, 1869, after a long illness, from paralysis.

Wesley and Eunice Kinne Bailey had six children. Of these, three survive at the present writing. The eldest is E. Prentice Bailey, born Aug. 15th, 1834, in the town of Manlius. At the age of nineteen he entered the office of the *Utica Daily Observer*, with which journal he has remained connected for more than a quarter of a century. In 1867 he became one of its owners, and from that date until the present he has held a place among the journalists of the State which need not here be estimated.

The second son, Ansel Kinne Bailey, was born in Erie Co., N. Y., Nov. 18th, 1835. With some rare qualifications for his future work, he succeeded his father as the editor of *The Teetotaller* in 1857, and accompanied him to Iowa in 1860, where the father and son started the *Decorah Republican*, which is now published by Ansel K. Bailey and Brother, the junior being Alvan Stewart Bailey, born in 1847, and named in honor of his father's early friend, before mentioned.

Wesley Bailey, leaving to these two sons a task to which they were fully adequate, retired from active business several years ago, but at the date this is written is in the enjoyment of good health and a happy old age. Honored, not alone by his kindred, but by all who know of his labors for the Master, and humanity.

E. P. B.

INDEX.

	Page.
Introduction	3
New England and New Englanders	7
The Military Tract	24
Genealogical Record	29
History of Cyrus Kinne	31
Family of Prentice Kinne	37
" Julius C. Kinne	43
Emerson Kinne	45
Family of Eunice Kinne	48
" Mason P. Kinne	51
" Elbridge Kinne	53
" N. Hildreth Kinne	55
" Emily Kinne	56
" Salome Kinne	57
Atlas Kinne	59
Family of Ansel E. Kinne	60
George N. Kinne	62

Family of Ezra Kinne.......................... 62
" Zachariah Kinne...................... 65
" Ethel Kinne.......................... 66
" Zebulon Kinne........................ 68
" Moses Kinne.......................... 70
" Joshua Kinne......................... 71
" Cyrus Kinne, jr...................... 75
" Japheth Kinne........................ 76
" Palmer Kinne......................... 77
" Rachel Kinne......................... 78
" Comfort Kinne........................ 79
Reminiscences of Moses Kinne, by his grandaughter,
    Julia Kinne................................ 80
Appendix.. 87
C. Mason Kinne.................................. 87
Wesley Bailey, by his son, E. P. Bailey............. 91

"	Ethel Kinne.................	6(
"	Zebulon Kinne..............	6.
"	Moses Kinne...............	7(
"	Joshua Kinne...............	7
"	Cyrus Kinne, jr.............	7!
"	Japheth Kinne..............	7(
"	Palmer Kinne...............	7
"	Rachel Kinne...............	7.
"	Comfort Kinne..............	7!

Reminiscences of Moses Kinne, by his granddaughter, Julia Kinne................. 8(

Appendix......................... 87

C. Mason Kinne................... 87

Wesley Bailey, by his son, E. P. Bailey........... 91

ERRATA.

In the 5th line from the bottom of page 78, for "Zechariah" read Cyrus.

At the close of page 44 insert the following:—"Helen M, only daughter of Julius C. Kinne, was married Feb. 3, 1857, to Dr. O. C. Williams of Mich."

In 20th line, on page 52, at the period insert "having married Lizzie K. D'Arcy of Boston, April 11, 1864,"

Page 56, fourth line from bottom, read Julius for "Jules." Page 70, first line, read sixth for "seventh."

ADDENDA.

Mrs Rachel W. Kinne, widow of Julius C. Kinne, died Dec. 12, 1881, at the residence of her son-in-law Dr. O. C. Williams, in Muskegon, Michigan.

Col. Emerson Kinne died at his residence in DeWitt, Dec. 20th, 1881, in the 78th year of his age.